BLENDING FAMILIES SUCCESSFULLY

HELPING PARENTS AND KIDS NAVIGATE THE CHALLENGES SO THAT EVERYONE ENDS UP HAPPY

GEORGE S. GLASS, MD, PA
WITH DAVID TABATSKY

SKYHORSE PUBLISHING

Skyhorse Publishing books may be purchased in bulk at special discounts for sales promotion, corporate gifts, fund-raising, or educational purposes. Special editions can also be created to specifications. For details, contact the Special Sales Department, Skyhorse Publishing, 307 West 36th Street, 11th Floor, New York, NY 10018 or info@skyhorsepublishing.com.

Skyhorse® and Skyhorse Publishing® are registered trademarks of Skyhorse Publishing, Inc.®, a Delaware corporation.

Visit our website at www.skyhorsepublishing.com.

10 9 8 7 6 5 4 3 2 1

Library of Congress Cataloging-in-Publication Data is available on file.

Cover design by Liz Driesbach

Print ISBN: 978-1-62914-431-3
Ebook ISBN: 978-1-62914-876-2

Printed in the United States of America

AUTHOR'S NOTE

Many former and current patients, colleagues and family members generously granted me permission to use their stories in this book for the purpose of helping others overcome similar situations. I have changed names, dates, and identifying characteristics for literary cohesion and to protect their privacy.

CONTENTS

PART FOUR
Becoming the Best Stepparent You Can Be

PART FIVE
Yours, Mine, and Ours: Troubleshooting for the Future

INTRODUCTION

Lessons My Family Taught Me

"Dad, I want to try parasailing before we go home," my thirteen-year-old son Frank announced on our last day of vacation. "Can you take me?"

"Yeah, me too," said Barry, the nine-year-old son of Donna, who I had been dating for eight months. "I really want to go."

"Oh?" I asked.

By that time, Donna and I were already entertaining thoughts of blending our families, so going to Mexico together for a long weekend seemed like a good idea. Her kids liked me; my son liked her, and equally important, Donna and I liked them back. Her thirteen-year-old daughter, Susan, was at camp, so it would just be the four of us, together like this for the first time.

The first three days were perfect. But on the last morning, just as we were finishing breakfast and heading off for our last few hours at the beach, Frank and Barry's request threw me for an unexpected loop.

"Barry, you're too little," I told him, slowly lifting my foot off the floor in the direction of my mouth. "And besides, I need some private time with Frank to do something special with my son."

Barry looked at his mother as if I'd swiped the perfect donut right off his plate. It was true; I wanted one last one-on-one activity with Frank before we left Mexico because under the terms of my divorce, the only extended time I had with him was in the summer. But Barry, like most nine-year-olds, was having none of it. He started crying, which immediately set off Donna.

"George, if we are going to build a family, everyone has to be treated equally," she told me. "No one gets his feelings hurt like this. We have to be inclusive."

I loved Donna and Barry and wanted our relationship to work. But for years, Frank and I had spent summers bonding as father and son, and he was about to go back to his mother for the school year. I was trying to explain that, but everything I said seemed to make things worse—for everyone. Here I was, a psychiatrist well trained to analyze other people's family dynamics but I couldn't do anything right with the people I cared for most.

Barry continued crying.

"You're being so self-centered," Donna snapped. "We're over!"

I was speechless, emotionally tied up in knots as I shifted between blaming the child she was protecting and wanting to cry myself because I was afraid I was losing the person I loved.

"You don't understand how sensitive Barry is right now," Donna said, getting up from the table to leave. "You can't just focus on your own son."

The rest of the morning sunk us all deeper into what felt at the time like an impossible hole. Donna wouldn't talk to me the whole ride to the airport. On the plane, we sat in different sections with our own child, intent on protecting them, while trying to convince ourselves that we didn't care enough about each other to make a real go of our relationship.

Luckily, cooler heads prevailed that day and Donna and I are happily married twenty-seven years later.

But I know I am a lucky man.

"I don't think it had anything to do with the kids," Donna explained to me recently. "You were the bad guy and kept trying to push it and you were treating the children differently. Barry was just a kid, and he and Frank got along great back then—and still do. You treating them differently is what got me so upset."

I was almost silly enough to bring up the age difference and the fact that Barry really was too small to parasail, but I've learned a few things over the years. In spite of my professional pedigree and ability to help others, when it's a question of my own family most of my acquired wisdom comes from my amazing wife. Besides all she's learned from earning a master's degree in education and teaching elementary school for many years, Donna has an uncanny ability to cut through all my analytical tendencies and get right to the heart of an issue.

"Come on George, get real."

I have heard that refrain from my wife endless times and I must admit it has probably never lost its relevance. It may only be topped by my children's familiar and favorite dressing down of their father.

"Dad, you don't understand anything; you are the worst psychiatrist in the world."

That's exactly how I felt when we returned from Mexico and Donna probably agreed. We originally looked for help in many forms to better understand where we came from, what we had been through, and how we could move forward and grow as a positive, blended family. We looked for books, but at that time we only found some technical psychiatric books, a lot of religious, spiritual tomes suggesting that a higher power wanted us to marry, and a few superficial cookbooks

(*The Family That Eats Together Stays Together*). Nothing fit our circumstances.

We talked to friends in similar situations, but most of them looked and sounded like the walking wounded. Some couples, in spite of their economic success and solid reputations in the community, disliked talking about their children from a first marriage and felt depressed about their struggle to build a blended family. We heard stories of kids turning to drugs, dropping out of college, and feeling lost into their twenties and thirties as a result of their parents' divorce. Sadly, a few parents had written off the children from their earlier marriages. What brought us down most was hearing an all-too-familiar refrain: "No matter what you do, the kids will never be happy."

This was unacceptable. So were the success stories we discovered that came without explanation: "I don't know why we've been so fortunate; we were just lucky." I knew there had to be help for me and Donna and all of those other families. Whether that meant learning new ways to facilitate healthy communication or defining why certain blended families functioned better than others, I felt determined to better understand myself, the needs of Donna and my family, and the children and parents who hadn't yet figured out that two families co-existing can be bigger and better.

This book is born out of that personal and professional quest.

On the personal side, I was the first one in my family to be divorced, and when everything in my life abruptly changed, I was living in Texas, far away from my roots, both physical and psychological. I was starting over, but despite being the leaver, within a short time, I felt like I was the damaged one, without a clue how to start over again. As a single and part-time father, I experienced feelings ranging from glee to guilt to boredom. Several years after my divorce, when my ex moved to California with my son, I became even more of a part-time dad, commuting on weekends and spending as much time with my son as possible during summer and school vacations.

When I met Donna, I was torn. On the one hand, she was someone I thought that I could be with, but she didn't fit most of the rules I had made for myself. I was terrified of starting over, especially because she had two children living primarily with her, and that meant I would be interacting with them on a regular basis. That image did not jive at all with how I was raised, believing in the fairy tale of Cinderella and Prince Charming (and their brood of perfect children) living happily ever after. I was petrified that I would become a sad character from *Fiddler on the Roof,* and that once I broke with tradition, everything else would fall apart.

Luckily, real life bested mythology on both accounts, and I soon came to realize that I had learned a lot during my ten-year mid-life adolescence while I was looking for Mr. Right. I made mistakes about how to date, how not to involve my child with someone until I was ready and what to look for in a new relationship. Altogether, my foibles actually set the stage for a positive, long-term relationship, but I should add that I didn't always follow my own best advice. However, I did develop the capacity to admit my mistakes, learn from them, and move on.

On a professional level, for over two decades I have witnessed people in my clinical practice—and now our kids' friends—repeating the same mistakes and finding themselves just as lost as we had been. With that in mind, I decided to detail some of my own experiences—numerous mistakes included—and what all of us have learned collectively. My

hope is that my personal chronicle and the anonymous anec-
dotes of my patients will help others in the process of building
a blended family.

Our path was full of bumps, potholes and unexpected
detours. It was only through a great deal of trial and error,
patience and forgiveness that we endured and prospered as a
family.

When we first got together, Donna's kids lived primarily with her. I tried to see my son every other weekend, but
traveling from Texas to California limited my visits to once a
month.

Donna and I got along well when it was just us and one
set of kids, in part because I essentially distanced myself and
let her do what she wanted. But when my son joined us, I
invariably tried to do what I wanted with him, which led to
fights that degenerated quickly into Donna and I pointing
out each other's shortcomings and failures as parents.

Case in point: If we were going out to a restaurant, we
would ask the children where they wanted to go. Two of them
always chose the same place, but the other always wanted to
go somewhere else. Typically, this conflict escalated into an
epic argument about one child being favored or one of us
parents repeating the bad behavior that led to our divorce.
It always upset everyone; even those who got to eat at their
favorite joint.

In spite of our struggles, Donna and I had two boys
together less than a year apart. Even after the three oldest kids
went to college we still faced the same battles when making
collective choices. The conversation would invariably turn to
an indictment of one of the kids or how one parent favored
one child over another—and why.

After years of dealing with the same issues we encoun-
tered with the children from our first marriages, Donna and

I realized that it didn't actually matter where we ate dinner; what each child needed was to feel listened to and special. Finally, after raising five children in a blended family, we had made a breakthrough!

It sounds like it should have been easy to figure out, but when you're living inside a merry-go-round of separate marital histories, misunderstood loyalties, satellite parents and a confused society, it's not easy to navigate a blended family. The labels we use only exacerbate the problem. "Step, half, real, natural, original and biological" have always sounded awkward and perplexing, for children and parents alike. If you're not my real mother, are you unreal? Is our family integrated, combined, quilted or synergized? My ex is now married with someone else's children. If I know them, what do I call them? Everyday conversation is peppered with attempts to codify, define and label what we are as individuals and families.

The twenty-first century family involves divorce, remarriage, and same-sex marriages. Quite often, children are the only link to a previous relationship, unwitting and painful reminders of a chaotic past or the fallout from a damaging divorce. Yet children and parents alike must find their way forward.

According to the National Center for Health Statistics, less than half of those who marry remain with their first spouse; fewer than fifty percent of children grow up with both biological parents, and at least one third of all Americans live more than fifty miles from where they grew up, a significant distance from their nuclear family or relatives.[1]

---

[1] Casey E. Copen, Ph.; Kimberly Daniels, PhD; Jonathan Vespa, Ph.; and William D. Mosher, PhD, "First Marriages in the United States: Data From the 2006–2010 National Survey of Family Growth," National Health Statistics Report, March 22, 2012, http://www.cdc.gov/nchs/data/nhsr/nhsr049.pdf.

These numbers are troubling and indicate a good chance that behind the closed doors of nearly half the households in America, someone is unhappy and needs help. In fact, there is probably someone you know struggling right now with some form of a broken marriage or embarking on a new one, fraught with challenges.

Most of us know couples that have started new families after a divorce. Many have found happiness with their new partner. But however ideal their new marriage seems from the outside, if their biological children are not integrated into their new family, there is a broken quality to the parent's inner life.

These parents may say "I did the best I could," or "I have new children now that make up for it," or "we're so happy together, just us." Despite those comments, they still feel guilt, depression and a sense of loss about how their children from the first marriage have not become happy, successful or capable of developing relationships of their own.

As a board certified psychiatrist and addiction specialist, I have treated families for more than thirty years, in the U.S. Navy, at several major university medical centers, and in private practice. I have treated some couples since before they had children and now treat their sons and daughters as adults.

My patients have taught me invaluable lessons about the link between divorce and issues of self-esteem, depression, substance abuse and relationship failures, which result from the break-up of a family. These same problems can occur with the introduction of a new spouse or children into a family. Unfortunately, parents in these situations often feel a need to choose between the new spouse and their own biological child, as if one could be lovingly preferred over the other.

These debilitating consequences have been well documented by mental health professionals, and given the incidence of divorce in our country, will only increase over time. But in spite of the belief many parents hold that the challenges of creating a blended family are insurmountable, I am convinced, based on my years of practice and my own personal journey, that in most instances, these challenges can be overcome.

This book is meant to help you do just that. Chapter by chapter, you will come to understand how you arrived at this juncture, how to begin a new, blended family and how to approach unavoidable dilemmas when they do occur. Keeping a healthy perspective will help you develop your own blended family in which every person feels appreciated and loved. Every family is different, but my own research shows that there are common denominators in raising children in blended families and the practical survival lessons I am offering in this book will help you and your family.

We all make mistakes; at least I do, according to my family. The key is to learn from them and to try to avoid them happening again. And if they do—and I say this from experience—you can turn your next crisis into a positive growth experience that helps every member of your family.

As I learned nearly three decades ago in Mexico, it is critical to be inclusive even when you don't consider it to be in your best interest at the time. Every child that survives a divorce and enters a new family is vulnerable. The children are usually the ones who get hurt the most by a divorce and the ones who will suffer the consequences for the rest of their life if you don't help them move on. After all, you are the adult, responsible for your families—old and new.

Blending a family is a process, which takes patience. It can take a long time to develop trust, acceptance and a willingness to overlook transgressions that in the beginning cause intense reactions to occur (look at what happened to us in Mexico, ouch!).

A friend with children from a first marriage in his twenties, and more with a second wife in his forties, once shared an observation with me.

"Having at least two sets of children is like eating bran: it may not keep you young and you may not live longer, but it sure feels that way."

If you take away one big idea from this book, I hope it is this: the most important role a parent can play in a blended family is to sustain a positive relationship with his or her own biological children while integrating them into the new family.

Here's to the good health of all of you.

PART ONE

TRANSITIONS

CHAPTER 1

HOW DID I GET HERE?

Most of us grow up with dreams, fantasies and plans for an idyllic life, complete with a happy-ever-after picture of a loving, intact family, with a spouse we honor and adore and healthy, thriving children who mean everything to us. Those images make us feel safe and secure. But as we know, approximately half of the time, our best intentions don't quite work out. What most often begins as a lovely marriage can turn into a most difficult divorce. Even in the best situation, splitting up a family affects everyone involved and may cause feelings of guilt, insecurity, anger and abandonment—just to mention a few.

For children and parents alike, divorce can threaten our desire to be listened to, included and loved. At best, these basic human needs are compromised when a family splits, and everyone, no matter what their unique personalities might be, is rendered vulnerable by the consequences of a divorce.

Children of any age often feel powerless, as if there is no longer stability, security or a place they can call their own. Parents encounter their own pain and confusion while simply trying to survive, and unfortunately, good parenting often becomes an almost secondary consideration. This mix of needy, troubled children with chaotic, anxious and depressed parents can become toxic and takes time to settle and adapt. It certainly does not offer the best foundation for picking a new partner or starting a new relationship.

It goes without saying (almost) that parents should re-examine their long-term goals before they actually break up a family, but realistically most of you reading this book have already made that leap and are trying to start over the best way possible.

But most of the time, that's quite a challenge.

"I was devastated," my wife, Donna, says, referring to her first marriage ending. "It was like a death. What was I going to do? I was alone with two children; nobody loved me anymore, and I hadn't really worked in more than fifteen years. I had to depend on someone with whom I had shared dreams and hopes, but who I knew I couldn't depend on any longer."

Donna's situation was not unique. I've treated countless patients over the years who have struggled with identical issues. Divorce marks the demise of a family as originally intended and can really feel like a death—for everyone. While there is nothing that compares to losing a child through actual death, the alienation a child (or parent) feels as a result of non-inclusion in a second family can remain an ongoing issue with life altering affects, no matter when it occurs or what the child's age may be.

But it doesn't have to be that way. One of the reasons I wrote this book is because I continue to see people making the same mistakes I've watched others, including myself, make over and over again.

A divorce attorney once told me, "You are only as happy as your unhappiest child." How depressing but true! Since I know from first-hand experience how bad the fallout from a divorce can be, I have committed myself to making sure that everyone I come in contact with—in my own family, in my practice and through this book—may reach their best potential for a happy and fulfilling life.

COPING WITH THE FALLOUT OF A DIVORCE

The realization that your marriage is over may occur gradually or abruptly. Weeks, months or even years of soul searching and perhaps multiple attempts at therapy and/or marriage counseling can lead to the knowledge that there is no viable chance for the two of you to remain together. Or it may happen out of the blue, as a result of a fight or when one person decides to leave.

We all know from watching too many soap operas and talk shows on television how crazy and irrational two people can behave inside the parameters of a marriage. While I always recommend that both parents make every effort possible to stay together for the benefit of their children, sometimes when the acrimony is too severe, it is best for families to break into two units, offering children a more peaceful everyday existence. But in any case, whether you are divorcing amicably or with rancor, whether it was a long time coming with multiple clues and hints along the way or an overnight and shocking calamity, it's happened. Your divorce is really happening!

You have to face a litany of evidence: the unexplained telephone calls, the credit card receipts that you didn't want to ask about, the curt explanations and those quick efforts to hide something on the computer. Or maybe it was all a gradual process of growing apart and the emotional distance kept growing bigger and bigger until you couldn't avoid admitting how unhappy, and frustrated and even angry you were, but didn't know how to talk about it, let alone make it better.

But through either of these scenarios or any variation you've experienced, you very well may have held onto the fantasy that your previous closeness, that spark you felt and shared when you first married, would magically return all by itself, without doing anything in particular, with no ugly confrontation or long, drawn out process of healing and reconciliation.

Like I said, some of us have been watching too much TV. Because as soon as one person talks to a lawyer and subsequently files for divorce, the train leaves the station as you once knew it and starts down the track, into territory that you could never have anticipated.

No one ever thinks he or she will have a severe car accident or become terribly ill or get a divorce. We always think it's something that happens to someone else—until it smacks us directly in the face and turns our lives upside down.

Despite the fact that attorneys are supposed to talk with their clients, and encourage them to try and work things out, either directly or through counseling and/or mediation, they invariably seem to point out everything negative that they possibly can about what can happen to an unhappy couple. While hardly knowing you and without ever having met your spouse, the person you trusted with everything—your life, your finances, your future, your children, and your hopes—he or she is portrayed as the villain, the one who has betrayed you, either directly with someone else, or emotionally, through ignorance or some other form of abandonment.

That is a worst case scenario, but it happens all too often. The attorney will point out that your spouse may have hidden the assets, is involved with someone else, will take the children, or that the new person he or she gets involved with later will somehow turn your children against you. Or worse, that your spouse not only doesn't want you, but doesn't want the children that you both planned for, cared for and shared either.

It's a horror show, and that's before you pay the retainer. Whatever your deepest fears were or how well you thought you knew your spouse after living with him or her for months or years, once the divorce process starts, you are suddenly shaken to the core about how little you knew. You start to wonder how he or she could do this to you, after you promised to cherish and be with each other forever. Those fears are often compounded by an attorney, trying to do his or her job by attempting to protect you fully, even though he or she does not know you, your spouse or your children, and your lives together.

Your fears may very well be enhanced by friends and relatives, some of whom may have been divorced, who start telling you stories about people they know or have heard of who were essentially left homeless, penniless, and childless by their ex and the lawyers.

This nightmare has nothing to do with the fantasy you had as a child or the happiness and hope you felt on your wedding day. Divorce is often worse than you could ever imagine. All the choices you make, or have made for you have real and lasting consequences—most of which seem less than optimal.

When it comes to anger, frustration, insecurity, paranoia and hopelessness, divorce is an equal opportunity devil. In many traditional home settings, women often feel unable to satisfy their children while struggling with their own need to make a living—forget trying to starta new life or relationship.

Men, by virtue of the court's natural bias towards mothers, suddenly realize that their involvement with their children can become very limited, and they can no longer pick and choose when and to what extent they will be involved, aside from providing financial support.

Pressures on both parents can pile up quite quickly with new schedules, fewer financial resources available, a compromised social life, and a whole new set of priorities for maintaining a positive relationship with your children.

THE BLAME GAME: ACCEPTING FAILURE

Divorce can render even the most secure person a mess. It creates vulnerability where it may not have ever existed. This often leads to feeling an unreasonable amount of guilt in doses that seem almost too much to bear.

"It's all my fault."

"I really messed up."

"I'm a failure."

Regardless of whether you are the leaver or the person left behind, it is hard not to accept some, if not all, of your part in the failure of your marriage. That acceptance may also lead you to consider yourself a personal failure as well. No matter how difficult your spouse is, no matter what you did, and no matter how hard you tried, clearly it wasn't enough to make your marriage work. At that point, as much as you may have tried to reconcile, agreed to go to counseling again, and give things one more try, you eventually realize that one of you isn't into it anymore, doesn't believe it will work, or just doesn't care enough anymore. And someone has to be blamed!

Even when you try to blame your spouse or focus on his or her shortcomings, of which he or she suddenly seems to have many, you know deep in your heart that you're only looking at half of the picture. In the middle of the night or in your truest moments, you admit to yourself that you bear a significant amount of the fault or blame. After all, when a marriage is over, it is your failure, too.

It can feel so bad, you don't want to leave your house and face the world. What will you tell your friends and colleagues at work? What about your family? Once you start sharing your situation, they may point out that they told you not to get involved with that person in the first place, that they knew he or she was not the right person for you. Seeing someone close to you being so unsupportive can often make it harder for you to try and work things out with your soon to be ex-spouse, whether it concerns complicated issues like money or more simple ones like visitation schedules.

It is incredibly sad when a child who loves both parents has to listen to a grandparent or a cousin disparage or criticize one parent because he or she left the marriage. Even if that child has been abandoned, it serves no purpose to compound the child's pain by badmouthing his or her parent.

The blame game does no good!

Alternately, if you, the self-anointed wounded one, are critical of your spouse, who is also the other parent, your friend or family member who may have liked him will see you as the difficult person, the one who could not be pleased or is at fault, and blame you for the divorce, or even push you to try and make it work. That may cause you to push back, and where will that leave you? Exhausted, divorced, and with fewer friends.

Marriage and divorce are very personal choices, which means you are the only one who can be responsible for them. It also means that trying to get others involved, to understand, or take one side or the other doesn't usually help—except of course when you need a supportive ear so you can talk about how badly you feel.

It's vital that you find a friend or family member you can talk to. Many people, regardless of whether they were the one leaving or the one left behind, consider their life to be markedly worse alone than it was when they were married. That feeling comes from much more than the financial hardships a divorce creates. Marriage provides a certain level of comfort in life when each of us feels that we are sharing our struggles, no matter how daunting they may become. So when a divorce occurs and you suddenly become a single parent, your stress level can shoot through the roof. The normal pressures of life become magnified, especially compared to what they were when you were married. Being a single parent can be overwhelming. For many, working all day and then coming home to take care of the children and the house, without another adult to help or the financial resources to get even part-time assistance, can easily be too much.

Someone has to be to blame!

I once asked a newly divorced single parent what she did for fun.

"Fun? What is that? On the nights and weekends when my ex gets the kids, I just relax or sleep and try to do catch up on all the chores I don't get to do when they are there. I may have dinner with a friend, or go out with another single mom and her kids to some kid activity, but I often don't have the energy for anything else."

Her answer was typical of the single mothers and fathers I see in my practice.

Their stress and fatigue is often increased if they are the primary caretaker, either by court order or by the de facto neglect of the other spouse. In either case, they have less and less time for themselves and have to do more and more as a result of their new role as head of the household. This can easily cause the primary caretaker parent to behave badly, to become angrier, more demanding and resentful of the other parent, and more abrupt and impatient with the children.

It can make you want to blame someone!

When it comes to gender, men and women may struggle with similar issues, depending on their circumstances, leaving them with the equal possibilities for blaming each other.

In the short run, men seem to fare better financially, as they tend to be the primary wage earners, but meeting the financial demands of a divorce is never easy. Newly single men often need to learn how to take care of the basics, like cooking, shopping, house cleaning and laundry. When you add trying to integrate confused, unhappy part-time children into the mix, it's no wonder that their patience can be pushed to the max. They become angry with the kids, blaming them for small inconveniences they would normally overlook, and mad at the ex for things she did or did not do in preparation for their time with the children. Like most of us, they are often clueless about how to reward, discipline or deal with an unhappy, demanding child. That's not easy, even in a happy marriage. When it's the dad who leaves, there is often a flurry of super-parenting, as if dad is campaigning to be anointed "Father of the Year," to prove once and for all that he is a good guy and doesn't want to neglect his children, despite the fact that he may have already done so. Gradually, it gets to men like this: the demands of paying child support, the new lifestyle of a single parent, and dealing with whiney, upset children who want to punish their parents for leaving. Taken together, this can often cause fathers to regress and emotionally withdraw, followed by spending less and less time with their kids or continually changing schedules to accommodate their own life.

And it's all so easy to justify when you can blame your choices on the divorce.

"He always tried to control me."

"I left because I couldn't be me."

"I just couldn't live the way I needed."

"She always did what she wanted anyway."

These are just some of the reasons people give for leaving their spouse and family in the process of a divorce. Unfortunately, once they have left and moved on with their life, many of these same people come to realize that they still haven't done any of the things they thought the other person prevented them from doing, or that they could have done many of those things if they had just communicated and asserted themselves, rather than blaming, or asking permission from the other.

"It was not until after we split that I realized that I could have gone out for lunch with girlfriends, had the occasional girl trip, or really done many of the things that I blamed him for not letting me do," said Jane, one of my clients not long ago. "Since the divorce, I didn't do those things at first, but I didn't have anyone to blame for my choices but myself. Now, I realize that if I had just put my foot down, I could have done those things anyway, maybe even in the context of a healthy, evolving marriage."

You can't play the blame game anymore once you're alone, looking in the mirror.

"I was shocked when I realized after the divorce that I could have just disagreed," said Peter, trying to describe to me what happened. "Or if she started to carry on, I could have just hung up the phone and called back later. By that time we both would have cooled down, and life could have gone on, but somehow, I didn't think I could live with her at the time, and it took living alone to finally get it."

The blame game has to end before it affects your kids.

Despite your attempts to reassure your children that the divorce is not their fault, the effects of your split will last a long time. Sure, you and your ex may go to great lengths to reassure yourselves that your children will be better with two divorced but happy parents rather than growing up in an unhappy household, but this mind game is more for your benefit than your children's. No matter how chaotic, unhappy or disinterested their parents may have been, children, particularly younger ones, prefer an intact family. For them, that was the norm, which means that when their parents split up, despite their comments to the contrary about how they expected it, or wanted you to do it, they're still surprised by the news. More than that, it almost always comes as a shock to them, and one that they will always remember as an event that changed their life.

I have heard many middle-aged adult patients tell me, as if it were yesterday, what they were wearing, which room they were in, and what they were told, when it happened—the divorce, the thing that rocked their world as a child. In my practice, I can often date the onset of an individual's loss of self-esteem, lack of motivation or poor performance in school to this point in their life, when a divorce changed everything.

When we consider this triangle of two parents and the child (or children) affected, we can equate it with a three-legged stool, trying to offer stability on at least one unsteady leg. How can anyone trust using that stool to sit on? Conversely, how can either parent or the children honestly trust each other, once a divorce has begun and the blame game begins?

There is another way.

DEFINING SUCCESS AND MOVING FORWARD

Success is relative in any endeavor and is not always obvious. But human nature dictates its necessity. In fact, our egos require it, no matter how reasonable it may or may not be to expect it, especially in challenging situations that are not entirely in our control. In remarriage involving children, success may not be easily defined or measured, and when it does occur, it's usually in small increments. But I have discovered that what can often be the elusive nature of success doesn't necessarily stop most people from hungering for it, in some cases, almost demanding it.

For example, among the many patients I've seen in my practice over the years, many of them believe that within weeks, if not months, of remarrying, the children involved should love everyone the same, and in some instances even call the new parent Mom or Dad.

Truthfully, that is naive and unrealistic. Personally and professionally, I evaluate success by how children of blended families are doing themselves, independent of their parents. Do they function well without us? Do they have positive relationships with each other, among themselves?

The answers to these questions will vary according to a host of factors, including the age of the children, geographic proximity to the divorced parents living away from home, and the length of time it took to blend the families together.

For me, as I view my family evolving, I see success among our children continuing on many levels. We all live in different parts of the country, look forward to family get-togethers, and are very appreciative that our grown children, who have limited time and a host of obligations, still choose to spend time with us. Donna and I are particularly happy when one of our children visits in a city where another one lives, and they choose to spend time together. In that moment, the sibling labels that society assigns just fade to nothingness and one can safely say that success has been achieved in a very real way. Each of our children has a strong relationship with us as well as with one another and has found his or her place in the world—in spite of us!

But I know I am lucky. Not everyone can claim success in this respect. Being a psychiatrist may have helped me sometimes to understand particular conflicts and given me the tools to create a supportive family environment, but when it comes to your own blended family, training in psychiatry is not a prerequisite to personal success, and at times it may even be a liability.

Our children have told me on numerous occasions, and will tell anyone who asks, that when I over-analyze a situation, I cause as many conflicts as I solve. Who am I to argue? I'm sure my children are right. Multiple degrees, certifications, advanced training and awards do not guarantee a thing when it comes to dealing with my own family. I am just like anyone else I know—flying by the seat of my pants, hoping to achieve an inkling of what I can safely call success.

However, I have found that occasionally, even after a family has been together for quite some time, something that seems to be a minor disturbing event can trigger off an emotional avalanche. It can happen suddenly, for no apparent reason, after months or even years of smooth sailing. You may be cast as the one to blame, but that doesn't mean you have failed, or that you are no longer appreciated. It could very well be a matter of lingering scars, and everyone needs to go back and clear the air, so that you can move on.

In spite of our best efforts to move on, every one of us who has been through a divorce carries at least a little bit of baggage. It's how we carry it that matters. If we at least acknowledge our mistakes and commit to working on ourselves, we can improve our chances of finding a better relationship. Along the way, we can do our best to be civil with our ex. Each of us has to realize that we will be involved with that person—the mother or father of our children—for a long, long time.

It also helps to remember that things can get worse and no one will really bail you out except you. There may be a knight on a white horse waiting around the corner or a princess in your future, pining just for you, but you won't find them sitting in your apartment, feeling sorry for you there. You need to pick yourself up and move on, one step at a time.

Listen to everyone along the way. Appreciate their feelings even if you don't agree, and then act with that understanding, rather than just out of your own idea of how things should be or how you think people should behave.

Don't let success or failure define you.

CHAPTER 2

STARTING OVER

As a patient once told me, "I don't really know how to date. It's been so long since I did that, and I hated it the first time around. My friends keep trying to fix me up, but I wouldn't even know what to do."

In the immediate aftermath of a divorce, dating seems terrifying while remarriage is a distant fantasy. Most people's half-hearted attempts to meet new partners are colored by fear, anxiety and depression, often accompanied by an overwhelming sense of being "damaged goods that no one would want." Between feeling guilty and considering yourself a failure because your marriage did not work out, you may not feel like an ideal dating candidate. Combine that with your ex-spouse's implication that you have "issues" or that you are the one with the "problem," and it's no wonder that you might think that no one "normal" would want to get involved with you. And then if you do meet someone, you may be afraid of getting hurt again, so why risk it? Have I mentioned the fact that you have kids, and that it can be an automatic deal breaker for some people?

The first time around, all of us were dating before we got married. Looking back, we were younger, naive, innocent, prone to parental influence and had a ready-made social network of family, religious, school and community connections. This time, our social network is different, if not antiquated, and full of married people. We know colleagues from work and other parents from our kid's activities, but most of our friends are married. As a single person, that means you may be the odd man, or woman out. Accordingly, we must branch out from our old contacts, forge new ones, and find different venues to meet people. But frequenting places just to meet people can be frustrating because when it doesn't happen, which is most of the time, it furthers your sense of being alone and a loser. Between the emotional awkwardness and the time constraints that single parenting usually includes, looking for someone new is a wish that often goes unfulfilled.

But it doesn't have to be that way. You can pursue a favorite activity to meet others with similar interests, be it a sport, a hobby or a cultural activity where at the very least you can enjoy your time even if you don't meet anyone special.

Realistically, meeting someone often breaks down to luck, friends, the internet, taking a risk and, maybe most of all, your own radiance when you start feeling good about yourself. Like many things in life, it seems to happen just when you least expect it.

After a divorce, many people shy away from old friends because of their own embarrassment about the break-up or because they think that their old friends may favor their ex. This is an opportunity to learn about yourself and to identify your most compassionate and supportive friends. Try to move through any paralyzing feelings you have and embrace your new beginnings.

In my case, I had a lot of friends who fixed me up on dates. The people they fixed me up with were usually very nice but none of them really fit whatever I thought I was looking for at the time. That's because I wasn't ready and hadn't figured out what I really wanted. My friends eventually stopped fixing me up because I guess they thought I was hopeless. They were just about right. I often would feel worse after a date than I'd feel if I hadn't gone out because I was already feeling badly about myself.

The key is trust, of yourself and your new friend, which can take time after a difficult divorce. One question you should ask is whether you are picking the same kind of person you picked before, which didn't work out, and whether or not you learned anything from that experience. It's essential that you figure that out through introspection, seeing a therapist, or talking it over with trusted friends. The answer to your questions will initially come from listening to your inner feelings. The more you are comfortable with yourself and realize you don't need someone to make you whole, the better equipped you will be to judge someone after you go out on a second or third date. Life is unpredictable, things change, and you really have to live it a day at a time. Maintain a long-range perspective of what you want, where you want to be, and whether the person you meet can help you get there. Make an honest assessment. If it is not going to work out or if you feel you have to really stretch to help it, perhaps you should cut your losses and move on before you become one of those people who spend too many years in a relationship that ultimately ends unsatisfactorily.

DATING VS. PARENTING

When beginning to date, it is good to establish boundaries between being a parent and having an adult social life. It is better at first to meet at a neutral location and for a predetermined amount of time. Dating outside the house lets children feel as if they have their parent's complete attention when you are home and protects them from the highs and lows of relationships that don't work out, not to mention people you are unsure of or find unreasonable. Children are naturally inquisitive and will involve themselves in your new dating life, so once you decide to mingle your dating and home life, you should feel committed to being with that person on an exclusive, ongoing basis.

Even divorced adults without children find it preferable to meet a date away from home, so that if it doesn't work out you can part amicably and in the least costly manner possible in terms of emotions, time, or money. That certainly beats being trapped for an awkward ride to either person's home. Until you are comfortable with someone, it is prudent to date away from your home, particularly if you have children. There are very few things more uncomfortable, if not downright creepy, than having someone you don't like show up at your home, trying to engage your children as a means of prolonging his or her relationship with you.

I learned all this painfully when I ended a relationship with a woman that Frank had gotten to know. She started to talk to him about how I was trying to end it, how important he was for her, and then she tried to get him to tell me how much she cared about him. Ultimately, everyone got hurt and it was because I exposed my son to someone before I was totally sure it was a good idea.

Dating can be difficult at any point but including your children certainly makes it more complex. Socializing with single, opposite sex parents of your children's friends often begins as a natural, non-threatening way to spend time with both your child and someone else. But the funny thing is your children will know more quickly than you what is really going on, and their unsolicited opinions about your romantic life may be positive or negative! But in all seriousness, dating within the circle of adults acquainted with your children can be risky because if and when the schoolyard romance fizzles, as they usually do, you and your children both can lose a valued friend. Awkward!

PRIORITIZE YOUR CHILDREN

Dating before your first marriage may have been a gradual process where the only distraction you experienced was work or school and the only time pressure was the biological clock or one set of parents pushing you to have grandkids. The second time around though, when you already have children from that first marriage, it will be much more difficult. Just arranging the logistics for what night, what time, where, and who babysits makes it very complex. All the planning and scheduling can make even a casual date an exhausting and expensive proposition, so moving slowly in developing a new relationship is usually better than jumping in too quickly.

Getting to know someone first lets you decide if you want to move forward. If things seem to be progressing positively then it could be time to involve your children. Not to be unromantic, but if either of you needs to get involved immediately and then gets the new person and your children involved quickly, it probably means that one of you is more desperate than you want to admit, or that the batteries in your biological clock are about to expire. Be honest about those issues! At the very least, you owe it to your children.

It is important to remember that your child may find your dating life-threatening. When children of a recent divorce see their parent focusing on someone else they may become frightened that they will be left again; this time by you. Depending on their age, they may be well aware that as their parent begins to focus time and energy on someone else rather than on them or on basic family activities, things may become very different. They may worry that these changes will hurt both of you, so they may react negatively. This can take the form of fault finding with the people you date, criticism of you, and whining or pleading as you prepare to go out. If you are thinking about adding someone into the mix, make sure it is the right person and that both of you are willing and able to do the work that will honor your child and make the relationship survive. Focusing on your child during this time will take care of a great deal of your challenges.

A patient of mine once told me that, "It was so awkward. I wouldn't go out during the week because the kids were home and had homework. If, on a rare occasion, I did, I would get back by ten to make sure they were settled. On the weekends, I would only go out when the kids were with their dad."

Because your children may feel threatened when you start dating after a divorce, it is easier and safer to socialize in situations where your children are uninvolved, not around, and know little about it. If you force the issue, they may pick fights over unimportant issues, find fault with your new boyfriend or girlfriend, complain to their other parent, or even fabricate stories about your new love interest.

Children want and need to feel that they remain their parent's primary focus, which means, more often than not, receiving our undivided attention. At certain ages, they will feel that their security is compromised when they are introduced to your new love interest. Although this doesn't mean that you need to stay home with them every single night, you should at least constantly remind them of their importance, and that meeting new people and developing a new adult social life will not come at their expense. In a way, you are role modeling because you are giving them the message that when something unpleasant happens in your life you need to pick up and move on, which may be something they will also need to do, particularly if they have had to change schools and make new friends.

As one child whose parents had recently divorced said, "I think all of my bad feelings from the divorce—the anger, the loneliness, the hurt, and the confusion—got worse when my parents, but especially my mom, tried to go on with their lives, whether it was dating or just going out with friends. I hated it when my mom went out on dates, although it didn't matter so much to me that my dad did. I think I felt it just wasn't right for my mom to be dating. This may have had something to do with the fact that I was thirteen and felt I should be out dating, not my mom."

The golden rule is always put your children first.

THE TORTOISE VS. THE HARE: FINDING THE RIGHT PACE

One night, nine years after my divorce, I was still single and looking for Mrs. Right at a cocktail party for singles. Donna walked into the room and once we started talking we discovered much in common: both of us had grown up in the same part of the country, lived in the same places at the same time with our first spouses, had children the same age, and we shared basic values regarding family, children, education, and even religion. But I was terrified to jump in. I kept thinking about her, but Donna was the one who actually called me first. It was only years later that I realized that while it was me who had started the conversation, it was in fact Donna who had picked me. She had never lived alone for any length of time, and after ten years of being single I was tired of telling my story. Fortunately, Donna felt comfortable from the start and thought I was nice. As she says, "We had so much in common it felt almost predestined." Lucky me!

Hopefully, at some point during your new round of dating, you will find someone you really like. But what's the hurry? If you fall in love—or think you have—too soon after the divorce it probably means that you haven't examined yourself sufficiently. What kind of person are you? What kind of partner are you really looking for? If you can't answer these questions clearly you are increasing your chances of ending up divorced again.

Slow down. As you begin to feel better about yourself and build self-confidence, a new relationship will happen. Don't despair! Single people find new soul mates every day, but first you have to learn to be happy with yourself. Once you do that you will notice many couples that have found each other after a divorce. You will realize that the same thing should—and probably will—happen for you again.

Pace is especially important when it comes to introducing children into your new relationship. Do it slowly. It may begin with a casual "hello" at the front door or in passing when your friend picks you up for a date. You may even have a short meal together, but when you begin to get everyone together, make it a gradual process.

Just like you didn't want to involve your parents when you first dated years ago, you shouldn't include your kids this time around, certainly not until you're sure that it's a serious and perhaps permanent relationship.

For children, when parents actually find someone new to be with, they have to get used to that person. Whether they like them or not, it is someone different and therefore a little scary. Many children feel like their mom or dad is being taken away from them.

One young patient told me the following:

"It was really awkward for us kids. We knew our mother obviously liked this guy, but we really didn't know what to say to him or what he was really like. He was so quiet that we could barely hear him when he talked. She had him over for dinner one night for his birthday, which was really weird. I couldn't understand almost anything he said so I just smiled stupidly and agreed with him. I don't know how they ever worked it out."

Once you have gotten comfortable with a new person, you will want to begin sharing the biggest part of your life— your children. If you ask your child when to do this, the most likely answer may be "never" or at least not until he or she leaves home for good and the parent is alone. Obviously, there is a discrepancy here and compromise is called for. That means, once again, taking it slow and putting your children first. If your new partner can't support that, you've chosen the wrong person. The last thing your kids need is to get attached to someone new and then be abandoned (again) if your new relationship doesn't work out. Nothing is gained by rushing a relationship between your new love interest and your children, but a lot can be lost.

When you finally decide to bring together your children, your love interest and his or her children, do something active and fun with clear time boundaries. The children all need to be aware of how long they need to be on their best behavior to make their parents happy, even if they don't really want to be there.

These get-togethers should not be seen as make-or-break scenarios, where any less than perfect behavior means that your new relationship will not work out. Keep things simple and try to just enjoy everyone and the experience, thereby avoiding situations where any less than perfect behavior—by a child or parent—can have any major repercussions. Pick a casual place where everyone can relax and have a good time. Avoid any formal situations. For example, a fancy holiday dinner with the grandparents is not a good first-time activity. Try a meal in a fast food restaurant, miniature golf, or the zoo. While it is natural that the children may not be eager for this whole thing to happen, make the best of it. And don't let whatever you do go on too long.

"I didn't really know what to say or do," a young girl told me in my office, describing what it was like when she first met her mother's new friend. "I knew Mom liked him, because she had him over for his birthday, cooked a good dinner, and bought him a present. He seemed nice enough, but I really couldn't wait for it to end so I could leave the table. I don't know what I would have done if we had been outside somewhere formal, where I couldn't leave after a while and go back to my room."

Whatever you do, do it slowly and with great care for your children's well-being

CHAPTER 3

BOUNDARIES: DEFINE AND RESPECT

"It is easy to be a father but very hard to be a dad."

This old adage speaks to the fact that all children have two biological parents, a fact that should be acknowledged in any serious "second-time-around" relationship. When the time comes, introduce the new person to your children as your friend and allow them to call him or her by first name. This is much better than using Mr. or Mrs., and is surely more appropriate than encouraging them to use Dad or Mom, even in cases where your child may have never met their other biological parent.

The person you introduce into their life may become the one to raise them and assume normal parental functions, but the child will be upset if they later discover that they have a different biological parent. At some time in the future, your child may decide to call the person Dad or Mom, but that choice should rest with your child. Trying to instantaneously create a new family or make your new friend feel accepted should never trump your child's wishes and comfort level.

"Adam never knew his real father, who left before he was born," a patient once told me, describing how she involved her new boyfriend with her son. "He was five years old, so I told him this is your new father. From now on we will call him 'Daddy.'"

Hopefully, Adam's response will not be, "You're not my father and I'm not going to call you 'Dad.' I already have a dad, and I'll find him one day."

Keep everyone's identities clear from the start and you will be served best later on when it comes to figuring out everyone's role in the new family dynamic. That means involving a new person slowly, keeping in mind the overriding concept that neither you nor your children should initially depend on or view this person as your surrogate. While in the short run, having someone there to help you with chores related to your kids may help out, it can add to their insecurity that you will abandon them, and if the relationship does not work out, you will be back doing your own chores again. In the beginning of a relationship, whether or not someone can take care of your children is not a good test of your compatibility together. When and if it doesn't work out, everyone may be hurt.

Keep things casual. Call people by their normal names and take your time.

HOW MANY PARENTS DOES ONE CHILD NEED?

Divorce may change a lot of things but it can never undo one central fact: the children you and your ex-spouse created will always be yours, in spite of their age and whether the courts determine them to be independent at age eighteen or twenty-one. No matter what, they will always be your responsibility—yours and your ex's—and no one else will ever quite assume that role, in spite of any involvement with your child.

This is a simple fact you must accept. But if for some reason you cannot care for, manage, or appropriately discipline your children, seek professional help to learn how you can. This may involve attending parenting classes, attempting counseling or getting help from your place of worship. If you need assistance getting your child to school or other activities, or someone to stay with them when you go out of town, find someone other than your new significant other to help you. Consider asking a neighbor, a friend, someone in a parents' cooperative group or another parent who has a child in your child's daycare. Don't use the man or woman you are beginning to get involved with as a babysitter, even if he or she offers to help.

In the early stages of a relationship, particularly as you are beginning to include your new friend within your family activities, it is not the time to have this person begin fulfilling parental tasks. While it may help you out in the short run, or appear to be a way to foster the new relationship, it is not fair to any of the parties: you, your friend or your children.

From your children's point of view, it conveys the message that this new adult may be more important to you than they are, making it seem as though you are delegating child-raising functions to a relative stranger. For your new friend, it may also be hurtful if he or she becomes attached to your child and the relationship—for whatever reason—ends. This often leads to unnecessary confusion, bad feelings and a sense of being used.

While it should seem obvious not to use your new significant other to care for your child, it can be an easy trap to fall into, as I ultimately found out myself once upon a time. It's a pattern of behavior I also hear repeatedly from my patients and colleagues. This is not to say that your children cannot spend any time at all with one of your friends, or even with his or her children. It is in fact often fun to share activities as you are getting to know each other.

For example, you pick up your friend's child after school, or drive him or her to an activity and then buy him or her dinner afterwards—all as a favor to your friend. The roles may be reversed at a later date. But that scenario is very different than coupling your child with the person you are currently dating. When you do things with a friend and his or her children, it tends to be child-centered and shows your child that you socialize, have friends, and have gone on with your life after divorce. It's also an effective way to break the pressure and tedium of single parenting your children.

My own story may be instructive. After my divorce, I made a real mistake in how I dealt with my first long-term girlfriend. My eight-year-old son, Frank, would come for the summer and as a single parent I was never quite sure what to do with him. I wasn't certain I could entertain him enough to guarantee that he had a great summer and would want to come back the next year. In addition, I had just gone into private practice and was working long hours. I thought it wasn't a bad thing to have my girlfriend help me out with my son. She could pick him up at camp occasionally or get a meal ready if I wasn't home. Keeping him company like that seemed harmless. She didn't have kids and was eager to jump in and help.

It was great in the beginning. But when the relationship ended, she tried to keep in contact with Frank, which I thought was a way to stay involved with me. I considered that to be manipulative, and it became upsetting for both my son and me. Besides, Frank had really liked her, which made the break-up hard for him to understand and even harder for me to explain why we were no longer doing things together.

In retrospect, it would have been much easier and more comfortable for everyone if I had managed the issues of his care by myself and kept her at a distance until I was really sure where we were going, if anywhere. An important lesson learned the hard way.

REDEFINING PARENT-CHILD RELATIONSHIPS

The person you ask to join you and share your life is really your friend. Someday, your children and this new person can become friends, but in the beginning he or she is there because of you, not your children. No matter how much your new love and your children seem to like each other, or how nice he or she may be, it is really not your child's responsibility to do things for this relative stranger.

This is different than the normal parent-child relationship where your children may help you out at times or help out their other biological parent with household chores. Housework, for example, is a central theme in many families because living responsibly together is a basic part of being a family. But that does not include asking your child to do things for your new significant other or having that person do things for your child. In the beginning, it's just not appropriate or reasonable.

Merging two families means getting to know and respect each other as people, and this can only happen a little bit at a time. Having your new friend be the nanny, teacher, or chauffeur, or treating a child as if he or she is the maid, butler, or babysitter does not move this process along and can easily make everyone resentful. Your child will continue to question why that person is there, why he or she has to do things for said person, and why you would require your own children to

do things for a relative newcomer. If you or your new partner want something done, one of you should do it—not the
children.

If your new friend has children that are younger than
yours, don't ask your children to take care of these children,
particularly if you want them to do that so you can go out.
If you want them to help out, offer to pay them for their ser-
vices. Otherwise, it will be seen as an imposition, implying
that their life and activities are unimportant and that they
are just an extension of you—all in all another unnecessary
source of resentment.

A patient shared a problem she was having with a new
friend and her son: "Why should I go upstairs and get his
book?" she reported her son complaining. "He can go get it
himself. He is your friend, not mine, and I didn't ask him to
come here and stay with us, or to leave his book upstairs."

When children are still recovering from their parents
splitting up, which means possibly for a long, long time, they
certainly don't need any more reason to feel resentment or a
sense of being manipulated. It's up to the adults to act like
adults, and not use their kids for the wrong reasons.

LIFE AND SEX BEFORE TYING THE KNOT—AGAIN

Because life is not perfect all of the time for anyone, the person
you are getting involved with probably has some issues, too,
including his or her own children, family of origin, finances,
ex-spouse, just to name a few! Enhancing each other's lives is
a hope, not a given. Even if that does happen, it is a process
that occurs over time as a result of small changes and minor
adaptations. Wish as you might, it is exceedingly rare for a
white knight or fairy godmother to instantly appear and make
everything perfect.

When a new person enters into your life, he or she may jump in aggressively to try and fix everything or save everyone, particularly if you allow it to happen or do not establish firm boundaries.

Or maybe it's you, attempting to right what you perceive to be a sinking ship. The friend you were trying to save and even his or her children may not have thought things were so bad or that they needed to be rescued. They may resent you as an outsider jumping in with a plan to make everything better—immediately.

If at some time the person you have become involved with asks for help then you can try to give it objectively up to a point that fits within your own comfort zone. But it's important to remember that whatever your friend's issues may be, they are not your issues. They belong to someone else who got into an unhappy situation. While your help may make things better, your efforts can also make things worse. It is someone else's life, someone else's family, someone else's children, and someone else's problem. If you are around long enough in the new relationship, your ideas, presence, style and role modeling may have a positive impact and everyone, including you, may benefit. But little will be gained by jumping in and telling anyone, particularly the children, what to do, or picking a fight with your new significant other's ex, who you may think is still causing problems. The reality is you may not be in a relationship with this person and his or her children long enough to make a significant difference, while they will be involved with each other forever. So despite pleas for help, some people really do not want to change or make things better. Their verbal or non-verbal requests to be rescued may be just how they try to get attention, which effectively undoes whatever you may try to do.

Most parents think they are doing a reasonably good job and know how they want to raise their children. Even when they have a sense that things are not going well, it is difficult for them to admit that they are doing a bad job, or need help. So if your new significant other doesn't ask for help, take a deep breath and don't offer any. That may be difficult; especially if you are an outsider observing a family situation that looks dysfunctional, troubled, or even chaotic and think that the parent you are involved with doesn't have a clue what to do or how to fix it. While you may be right in your assessment of the issues, your effort to jump in, take over, rescue, or redirect everyone may actually make everything worse. Resist your first impulse to provide unsolicited advice or interfere with the hope of saving someone you care about. Instead, ask for the biological parent's opinion of how the situation should be handled. He or she will probably have an idea, even if it cannot be expressed properly at the time, particularly in the middle of a crisis. More likely than not, this is not the first catastrophe that parent and child have faced, and your interference may only make things worse.

An adolescent patient who was brought to me for depression and drug use described what happened in his family. "I really liked my dad's girlfriend at first. She would do things with me like pick me up after school, cook, and sometimes get him to take me places that he wouldn't have done before. Then she started telling me what to do, and telling my dad what he should and shouldn't do with me. She even called me spoiled. I probably was, but I didn't need to hear that from her, and I got really upset about it. Ultimately I resented her. She really shouldn't have jumped in so quickly, even if we both needed it. She started putting down rules and punishments on me when my dad wasn't around, and when I finally told him, he didn't do anything. That is when things really got bad for me."

We should learn from our children—the ones we bring directly into the world and those we care for professionally, as teachers, clergy and therapists. Their struggles can inform our personal lives and make theirs better as a result.

So no matter what the problems may be, take things slowly, observe what has been going on, and give your advice or input in a thoughtful, non-intrusive manner—if and when you are asked. In that case, ask the biological parent: how were things handled in the past, why were they handled that way, how should things be handled this time around and what can you do to help? The parent and the children will both be appreciative if you follow this path. And, if the situation doesn't work out, you won't be the scapegoat that everyone jumps on to blame.

As the two of you become more involved and begin thinking about marriage, you may consider living together. This usually means that the divorce has been finalized and you can take your relationship to another level—when the children are not around. But living together may affect your legal situation. Will your ex-spouse be upset if his or her children are with you when you are cohabiting with someone else? You may think that no one should care who you sleep with or live with if you are a consenting adult. That may be true when you are single, but it is very different when you have children. Your living with someone else affects everyone, but particularly your children. To a child, the fact that a parent is living with someone further pushes the realization that his or her original family unit exists no more. That's a tough pill for many children to swallow. It also makes them aware, at least by a certain age, that there is a sexual aspect to their parent's life. In the early stages of living with your new love, your children may resent it. If they are aware of you sleeping together, which they usually are, it can even cause them to see sex as a bad thing, or consider it to be the reason that their original family broke down. That could make it harder in the future when they try to have their own relationships.

In general, until your plans for the new marriage are well underway, it is probably a good idea to not move in together, or at least to stay apart or live separately when the children are with you. Whether they are younger or in their adolescent years should not make a difference. The children may know that you stay at your friend's house when they are not with you, but that is very different than the two of you being together in their face, all the time. Adolescents may even get the message that sex and living together is permissible for everyone, including them, which clearly is not the message most parents prefer sending.

"We did not think that living together was a big deal after we started dating," a patient told me recently. "The children did not seem to care and things were pretty good for a while. Ultimately, we got married, which seemed to legitimize it and it really wasn't an issue until my daughter turned sixteen and wanted to have her boyfriend live with us. He was having problems with his parents and was a pretty nice kid, but that just didn't seem reasonable to me. Everyone went ballistic and my daughter kept pointing out that we had done it so why couldn't she? We finally resolved it, but in retrospect it would have been a lot easier if we had just postponed living together a little longer."

Children seem to have radar for when their parent's new relationship becomes sexual. Even when your sexuality is not flaunted or displayed in front of them, the energy surrounding it changes how your children perceive the interplay between this new person and you, their parent. At some level, they may recognize that your life has an intense dimension that is threatening for them and they may also recognize that your new friend has more importance to you than your other friends.

"Whenever this one guy came over," a young patient reports, "Mom would do this funny thing with her lip. I thought it was really weird, but I couldn't tell her because she thought she was being cool."

Children may sense that a new person is replacing their own parent, even when this is not the case, which may certainly cause them to dislike your new friend. They note when their parent begins to focus on the appearance and sexual aspects of the new person. Later in life, they may view being sexual or attractive as a negative, in part as a response to feeling that these qualities were important to their parent, and feel as though the added sexual tension may cause the new person to replace them in your life. This all points out again how important it is to try and keep that person, if not that aspect of the relationship, separate until you are sure that you want him or her involved in your child's life.

No matter what, no matter how anxious you are to begin a complete life with your new love, you must love your children before you can love anyone else.

LESSONS LEARNED

1. Re-examine long-term goals before they actually break up your family.

2. Make every effort possible to stay together for the benefit of your children.

3. Admit to yourself that you bear a significant amount of the fault or blame.

4. Badmouthing the other parent serves no purpose and only hurts your children.

5. You are the only one responsible for your choices.

6. Find a friend or family member you can talk to.

7. The blame game has to end before it affects your kids.

8. Listen to everyone.

9. Appreciate their opinions even if you don't agree.

10. Don't let success or failure define you.

JOINING FAMILIES: WHAT TO EXPECT WHEN YOU REMARRY

CHAPTER 4

MARRIED WITH CHILDREN: YOUR REAL-LIFE VERSION

To say that there are dramatic differences between a person's first and second wedding is a decided understatement. First weddings are most often an expected and welcome passage in life, something that traditional society embraces. For many women, it is a dream come true and their chance to be Princess-for-a-Day. Weddings are also a showcase of sorts for parents who wish to make a statement to their friends, while acknowledging how they have evolved as a family. Any reference to children is usually directed toward the bride and groom, with the occasional uncle toasting to their good fortune and successful procreation. In the first marriage for both parties, even when one or both sets of their parents are divorced, the slate is clean because there are no children involved.

But in the case of second marriages that include the bride and/or groom's respective children, the landscape is very different and certainly more complex. When friends and family refer to "the children," they are all too often implying a sort of "baggage" that is perceived to be part of the overall marital package, but the issue is how to involve them all so they do not seem, or become, unwanted baggage.

Second weddings are usually orchestrated with much less pageantry, without any statements by the couple's parents or toasts and winks hinting at enlarging what may already seem to be an oversized family.

KEEPING YOUR KIDS IN THE LOOP

In a very real way, the prospect of another failed marriage is always a concern as a couple embarks on this new adventure. Any past failures do not need to be advertised by another large celebration. The second time around, friends and peers are more important to the couple getting married, particularly those who may have helped and supported the single divorced parents during their ongoing struggle and search for someone new. Beyond the joyful hopes for a better future, it can be a humbling occasion.

Perhaps the biggest question that arises when planning such an event is what to do with the new bride and groom's own children. It's good if this question is asked early on and discussed frequently because it is extremely important.

No matter how complicated a couple's situation may be the answer is simple. The wedding must be viewed and handled as if it's for the children as much as it is for their parents. This second time around, it is not by any means the grandparents' wedding. Since a wedding is a celebration of starting something new, which should be wonderful, it also means that it is the end of something old (i.e., the original family that the children have known since they were born). Therefore, both the bride and groom's children must be considered from the beginning of the process and, if they wish, be included in the ceremony.

This means that you should tell your children as soon as you know that you intend to get married. It is much better that they hear it from you rather than from someone else. They need time to grieve the end of their biological family before they can move on and greet a new life. Whatever their age, your marriage to someone new will affect them just as much, as it will affect you, if not more.

A parent's new marriage will impact almost everything in the life of a little child, from where and how he or she lives to how he or she is treated. It will also impact how much time each biological parent gets to spend with the child and depending on the amount of time the child does spend with each parent, he or she may be more comfortable with one than with the other. The new marriage will ultimately affect the course of a young kid's relationship with both parents. Not surprisingly, the first concern of the children is usually how it will affect them. Most fear they will be displaced—again—and are left to wonder whether the new marriage will mean that they will lose another parent.

It should come as no surprised that some children become negative as the marriage date approaches, even though they seem to like the person you chose, and have been supportive of the idea of you getting married. This negative response is natural and often occurs when anyone faces a significant change in life. Don't be too discouraged or change your plans.

Your children will ask questions:

"What will happen to me?"

"Where will I fit in?"

"Will I fit in?"

"Is there a place for me?"

These questions are reasonable and should be expected of children of any age suddenly confronted by such a monumental change. They should be constantly reassured that you will love them despite the changes and that there is definitely a place for them in your new family.

One of the best ways to point out how integral they are to your new family is to keep them informed about what is going on and involve them in the planning as soon as you can. This includes much more than merely planning the wedding, a one-day affair.

It's more about what the ongoing living arrangements will be—what, if any, effect it will have on where they go to school, who their friends will be and what new family obligations they will need to fulfill.

"I guess I knew they were going to get married," one of my younger patients told me. "Mom started to talk about what would happen. She kept telling us that she loved us, and that everything would be the same, and it got to be kind of annoying because we knew it anyway, but in a funny way, it also made us feel better just to hear it again. Our dad was really okay with it. He was so busy with his own social life that it didn't seem to make much difference to him, and mom's new husband was nice to us, and not nasty to him, which was really all he cared about anyway. I mean, I was still a little shocked and upset when it really happened, but I think I felt better about it than I would have, otherwise. Her constant communication really helped."

A child's anxiety about one of his or her parents marrying someone else becomes even worse when the new person also has children of his or her own. For the anxious child, this means that this new blended family means a package deal: stepsiblings on top of a stepparent. It suggests a new hierarchy emerging, with a whole new set of questions.

"Who will you care about more, your new wife's kids or me?"

"What loyalty will your new partner have to me?"

"Two parents already seems like a lot. How do I manage three?"

In the eyes of a child, your new marriage into an already existing family can look like an emerging turf war. Will one of these adults become the lead or Alpha parent and put their children ahead of the other person's? Kids know that the new adult in the mix doesn't have a biological or historical connection to them, so they figure why should that person care about them or take their side when any problem comes up? Children worry that if their biological parents split up and one parent has already left them, then why won't this new adult, with no biological connection to them, also leave at some point? Given such fears, it's natural that kids worry about getting too attached to this new person who might also leave them. It is also natural that at the last minute they may want to fight to prevent the marriage, and keep the status quo they had, which may not have been great, but was at least familiar.

An adult's second marriage is also a child's potential prescription for anxiety, fear of abandonment, loss of family bonding, and the end of previous experiences with known reality. This sounds terribly daunting, and in some cases, it is. The antidote is quite simple: constant love and reassurance that the child will not be replaced by either a new stepparent or that person's children. The process of reassurance should begin before the divorce, and should continue long after the marriage ceremony, with the understanding that at times of future stress, like when new children are added and anxieties reappear, children will need additional support.

Tell your child again and again that he or she is loved, that there is a place for him or her in your life and in your new family, and that he or she is important to everyone. Keep this dialogue going until he or she starts to say, "Yeah, I know that you love me. Back off, I'm getting tired of hearing it, and it's embarrassing in front of my friends." Then, keep on telling him or her, because everyone, even you, likes to know that they are important, wanted and cared for.

PLANNING THE WEDDING

My own experience of getting married for the second time was mixed. In the first place, we were so glad to be able to finally get married. Once Donna's divorce was finalized, we arranged a date during a holiday when we knew that all the children would be there, and when a few other people, like our parents, could come. We figured that while we should ultimately make our own plans, involving both sets of children in the process would help make everyone feel more secure and get the process moving in a collaborative direction. Plus, your children know you better than almost anyone else and Donna and I thought they would have some good ideas to make the whole process even more fun.

As we were making up the plans for a reception after the wedding, we let them help us pick some of the appetizers, which they seemed to like. They had ideas about what everyone preferred.

One story sticks out for me, in particular, because it reminds me so much of our own experience.

"I was really upset when my mom got married, but I didn't realize how upset I was until the actual wedding. I couldn't tell her beforehand because she seemed so excited, and I was glad that I had a part in the actual ceremony. But in the middle of it, I ended up crying. I realized it was the end of my old family, I really didn't know what would happen, and I wasn't sure that I wanted anything to change. The planning for the wedding helped me a little, but being there really made me realize it all at once. I was really glad though that I went."

Children from both sides should not only be involved in planning the wedding, but should also have a role in the actual ceremony. One size does not fit all, but making a child the Best Man or Maid of Honor, a Bride's Maid, a Groomsman, a Ring Bearer or a Flower Girl may certainly do the trick. You can even create a role that is not part of a traditional ceremony. Even if the children are young, they can still participate in what will remain a very important event for them well into the future. Minor children in particular will be affected, especially those who have been solely dependent on their biological parent for some time and will continue to be for a significant time after your wedding. Very little children have memories later in their life about important events they were involved in and no child is too young to be included. You need to make major efforts to involve yours and your new spouse's children—even the rebellious ones and those who have been acting out to express their unhappiness about what is about to occur. After all, if you manage it right and succeed in your new marriage they will come around eventually and participate with everyone else.

I have seen what happens when children are not included and it's not a good thing. Exclusion is basically equivalent to punishing them for expressing how they feel at the time, which is usually unhappiness about the break-up of their family and the fact that you may no longer spend time focusing exclusively on them. Even if you don't agree, you need to listen to what they are saying because in their view, they may feel that you have made their life worse because of your new plans. Not including them because they are unhappy tells them that their parent's love for them is conditional, and can be lost, just like their original family. Your effort to include them makes a statement to the children, to your new spouse, and to everyone else that your children matter!

Many second marriages break up because a parent feels they need to decide between their new spouse and their child, which will ultimately become an intolerable situation. You can avoid that pitfall if you involve your children in the primary stages of these changes.

When Donna and I got married, we gave the kids important parts to play. Frank was the Best Man, Susan was the Maid of Honor, and Barry was the Ring Bearer. It didn't keep them from being sad and upset, but they all knew that they were important to us, and had a vital place in our new lives.

After the ceremony, we all went to a small hotel for the reception. It was nice, given that we were paying for the whole thing this time, and considering that we had so many other uses for the money, like living expenses and our kids, it felt especially rewarding to make our own choices about how to celebrate our marriage. At that point in our lives, we knew that if we didn't have a good time and enjoy our own wedding, we were really in trouble.

However, our euphoria was short-lived. Barry, who was ten years old at the time, had been upset and crying during the ceremony, and for some reason, he was left unsupervised at the party. We discovered when we got home that he had been nipping on leftover cocktails and either fell asleep or passed out when he got home. Susan, fourteen years old and my new stepdaughter, didn't know what to do with her instant stepbrother, and with Barry effectively unable to talk, we found her awkwardly watching TV. Frank, also fourteen, was unsure of how to relate to his instant stepsiblings, so he awkwardly continued lifting weights in the same room while Susan watched TV and Barry slumped across the couch. Nobody talked to each other. So much for instant blending. For me, aside from marrying the woman I loved, it seemed like a regular night. Teenagers acting like teenagers. Barry was home safely and I would take care of him in the morning. Mostly, I looked forward to the next day and taking our whole family to lunch.

COPING WITH RESISTANCE AND EASING ANXIETIES

While you might think your second marriage is the best thing that has ever happened to you there is no guarantee your child will see it that way. Their solid and stable world, which was thrown into chaos as a result of the divorce, may have finally settled down, but is about to be thrown into turmoil once again.

Your new marriage finalizes the end of what your children have known as their only family, and squishes any dreams of it ever being reestablished. Unfortunately, the only control they can feel over what is happening may be expressed through negativity. From your children's point of view, your new marriage is the funeral of the only family they have ever known—their own biological family. What can they do to let you know how unhappy they are about that loss? Your children may have tried to tell you a hundred times, in many different ways, how upset they are about their family ending, but despite their input, you and their other parent are still divorced. Now, although they may have told you they are unhappy, or don't want you to get remarried and move your life forward, you are going through with it anyway. Their conclusion is that you either did not hear them, paid no attention or don't care, because they cannot see any other explanation for what you are doing.

There are many different ways children tell you they are sad or unhappy and would like to stop a process you see as moving on with your life. The child may suddenly tell you they do not like the person you are involved with, or think you should have married someone else. One very basic way is to tell you that they will not attend your wedding, or if they must come, they will not participate. These statements are ways for them to let you know they are unhappy, and that they feel they have no control over a major part of their life.

Remember that you are the parent, and despite their negativity, don't react out of hurt and anger from your perceived lack of support. Continue reaching out and include them in your plans because you are theoretically the more mature one in the relationship. Give them the opportunity to change their mind at the last minute, as we all have done throughout our lives without being penalized for our indecision. This prevents you from making a decision that you might later regret. It's a chance for everyone to learn from mistakes. This means that they will know you tried to make them part of the process, the celebration and the new family.

Even if they do not come, keep trying to reach out and include them in your life as it goes forward. Not doing so sets the stage for bad feelings on both sides, and may make it even harder to include them later. They may think that you will remain angry because they didn't attend the wedding, or be embarrassed about what they later view as their own bad behavior. Your new spouse may be hurt and angry, and help drive a wedge between you and your child, which will make it even harder in the future to work things out. The easiest thing is to try and include them. It really does not hurt anyone, but it does lay the groundwork for things to improve later. No matter what, leave the door open.

CHAPTER 5

COMMUNICATING WITH YOUR EX

The most important person in your child's life, besides you, is their other biological parent, your ex-spouse. You and this person were involved for some period of time and had children together. If you are honest, your ex did have some good qualities, which is why you two dated, got married, and stayed together for as long as you did. Ideally, you and your ex should have reasonable interactions and communication, at least around your children. Though, if this had been great in the past, you two would most likely still be together, instead of divorced.

TO INVITE OR NOT TO INVITE

Your former spouse should not be the last person to know that you are getting married, and yet that is often what happens. There are many reasons people give for not notifying their ex, but many of these excuses do not justify their decision. Some people feel that their ex is no longer involved in their life, and others think their former spouse will try to sabotage their new relationship before it has a chance to begin. Some still feel their ex will try to control them, or continue to make their life miserable, as they did while they were married. So why give your ex the opportunity? Don't say anything!

Time out. Regardless of how your relationship has changed, your ex should be informed about what you are planning. If your children spend equal time with both parents, your ex-spouse will need to know about your new marriage to better meet the needs of your mutual children.

HE/SHE IS YOUR CHILDREN'S OTHER PARENT

While you may think you have good reasons for not informing your ex of your pending marriage, he or she needs to be prepared in advance about how this change will affect the children you share. Your children will react to a new marriage for a long time, and their other parent—your ex—will notice those reactions, but may have no clue what is going on unless you say something in advance. If you don't say anything, your ex will not know how to respond to the child's behavior and needs, which is unfair because both of you should have your child's best interests in mind. The ex needs to know what is going on to understand your shared child's behavior, and effectively intervene to help if that becomes necessary. Tell your ex. It is much better if he or she hears it from you than second hand from someone else. Or even worse from the children.

RESPECTING HISTORY

Whatever your relationship, you and your ex will ultimately be involved with these children for a long time. The harder you work on improving your relationship with that person, the better things will go for you, your former spouse and your children. Try to take the high road, and treat your ex as a real person, even if you are not treated that way currently or while you two were married. If nothing else, your children will benefit.

From my experience, it seems reasonable to tell your ex-spouse about the same time you tell your children, even though you have all the fears and concerns that he or she will interfere, meddle, or try to sabotage what you are doing. If you and your soon-to-be new spouse are committed, it should really not make a difference. In fact it may improve your relationship because you are asserting your independence, showing you are moving on. This also tells your ex that you want and need support for the children you have together. In general it is better to tell your ex alone, rather than with your children present, or with your new, soon-to-be spouse. After all, you are not asking permission, you are just informing this person, and helping everyone move on.

It is probably also best to frame the discussion around how your pending nuptials could affect your mutual children. Explain that the children may behave strangely and may need support from their other biological parent. In this manner, you are focusing on what is best for the children, and your ex's involvement in that rather than making it about you, and your past relationship.

The ex-spouse, after some initial shock, may react in several different ways, which are detailed below, but take one of several scenarios. The ideal one is that of supportiveness, and encouragement, wishing everyone well. The next most optimal one is trying to talk you out of it, trying to rekindle the old relationship one last time or even suggesting you both go back into relationship counseling. This may seem romantic but if your first marriage was meant to work, it probably would have.

Sometimes, an ex can become negative. At best, he or she will ask you if you know what you are doing and then may threaten to take the children, change the custody arrangement or in some manner disturb the financial agreement you had previously agreed to. All of these are efforts to control and/or manipulate you and really should have no impact on what you are planning. If your soon-to-be spouse does not have a prison record or a history of child molestation then there is little reason for a custody arrangement to be changed. If the finances were detailed in a divorce decree, there isn't much one can do to change that agreement. Your ex can certainly tell the children bad things about the new person in your life, but if the children already know this person that may be ineffective, and your ex's efforts may backfire.

A patient told me a sad story a few years ago.

"I can't believe it. She's getting married again, and it's like the old marriage is hardly over, and the body's not even cold. What's worse is that the children knew, but didn't say anything to me. The way I found out was that our youngest child began having trouble in school. He was getting into fights, his marks were falling, and he just seemed unhappy and angry all the time. He didn't say anything to me until we got a call from the counselor and had a conference at school. Then, right there in the middle of the conference, my ex-wife tells the counselor that she's getting married again, but that it was okay because all the children like her new husband. My son is still in therapy, but it is a long road back and a lot of it could have been avoided."

All in all, it really is better to tell your ex and to ask for support with the children in the transition.

CHAPTER 6

WHAT'S A HONEYMOON THE SECOND TIME AROUND?

In the months leading up to our wedding, Donna and I had essentially been living together with our kids except for the occasional visitations they would have with their other biological parent. (This is one of those doctor-like do as I say, but not as I have done points.) We felt like we really needed a break to have a little space for ourselves. We spent a week in Mexico shortly after the wedding—just the two of us—and had a really great time. It was our first experience not having to schedule around our kids, which in our case involved three young adolescents. In retrospect, it was really a great way to start everything off. In some ways, it was better than the honeymoon we each had experienced from our first marriages because this time we really needed a break—together.

THE CEREMONY'S OVER: NOW WHAT?

In second marriages, the tradition of taking off immediately after the party for some exotic destination is often merely a fantasy. Arranging time for a honeymoon can be a complex affair requiring extensive planning to find a time that fits both the work and visitation schedules of everyone: the newlyweds, their exes, and all the children. Many people skip the honeymoon because these negotiations can be too complex. Others just want to save money or can't find anyone to take care of the children while they go away.

Despite the complexity involved in actually making the arrangements, it is usually good to take some type of a break, even if it is short and to a place nearby. This is true, even if everyone including the children has been living together before the wedding. A honeymoon is an event that helps clearly delineate for everyone the end of one life and the beginning of another. It is important that something be done to celebrate and mark this transition. Whether or not the children go along, or how luxurious the trip turns out to be is less crucial. While it is normally important to try and involve the children in most things, this is a time to "chill out" without them, even for a day.

Shortly after our wedding and honeymoon, we took our three kids on a Christmas vacation to a place that Donna had gone to many times before. On our last night we went to her favorite restaurant. After dinner Barry and Frank went to play backgammon. Barry began to cry and said that he was upset because he used to do that with his dad every year in the very same place. As we started talking about it, he grew sadder, Susan withdrew and Frank became silent and tense. It was clear that Donna's kids were being reminded of what used to be and that Frank, who had never talked much about his own feelings, wasn't quite sure how to deal with it. Gradually, as we talked, cried and hugged, things seemed to get a little better for everyone, although we all talked about how it would never be the same. Each of us had to learn something new about change, and above all, Donna and I tried to encourage our children to stay open and not fear it.

PLANNING THE NEXT STEPS

As soon as the ceremony ends and the honeymoon is over, things can get very complicated, even if everything seemed to be flowing smoothly up until that time. A newly married couple creating a new blended family rarely has an opportunity to reflect, let alone make plans in isolation because children from one or both spouse's previous marriages are always there and in need of some kind of attention. In spite of that, take time with your spouse to appreciate what you have accomplished and plan for your future. But beware. Children are supposed to be flexible, impressionable and eager for a new and better life, but they frequently are not in the beginning. They are often very unhappy about the changes and express their unhappiness in many ways. Children are often a reminder of your previous families. They may try their best to perpetuate long-standing traditions while verbally reminding everyone of how it was "better in the olden days."

WHAT TO DO WHEN NOT EVERYONE WANTS TO CELEBRATE

As a new couple begins to establish their own patterns, their children will most likely fight this process. They are being dragged, kicking and screaming, into a future they are not sure they want to join. They often see no reason for the marriage, are upset by any change, and continually remind everyone verbally and behaviorally that not only was it different before, but they liked it better that way. In some ways, this can be almost a replay of a first marriage, where the couple's parents and in-laws carried around the old values and continually reminded the couple of them. The children in the second marriage are the reincarnation of the in-laws from the first one, and are always quick to point out everything that is not right or was done differently or better in the past.

This disruption continues for some time, with the child carrying around their old biological family's values and memories, while resenting the need to give some of them up. Gradually, there will be fewer instances where this occurs, and as they are successfully resolved new ones should occur less frequently and without so much emotional intensity. As that happens, the children's reactions will change when they realize that things may be better and that they have input into the new family. In the beginning though, time is a luxury that no one has. Children are often less impressionable than everyone thinks them to be. So don't be shocked if these situations occasionally come up in the future.

It was shocking to me in the beginning that Donna would ask the kids what they wanted to do and then listen to their input. I grew up with parents deciding everything and the kids going along with it, albeit resentfully. I kept saying, "But you keep treating them like real people, not kids." There I was, a professionally trained psychiatrist, learning something new yet again.

LESSONS LEARNED

1. Tell the children what you are planning and reassure them of their importance.
2. Involve all of the children in the wedding plans and the actual ceremony.
3. Make sure that each child has a role in the wedding.
4. Include the children, even if they say they don't want to be included.
5. Continue reaching out to the children, even if they say they don't want to be involved.
6. Inform ex-spouses that you are getting married.
7. Even a simple honeymoon helps demarcate the past and the new relationship.
8. When the ring goes on, things change for everyone.
9. After the wedding, begin new family rituals.
10. Be patient.

GROWING PAINS

CHAPTER 7

RULES TO LIVE BY

Being a parent is notoriously difficult, even in a traditional family with two biological parents raising a toddler, helping a pre-adolescent navigate the transition from home to the outside world and absorbing the brunt of a teenager's angst as he or she tries to find a place in society. As this process unfolds, parents must also transition from carefree, irresponsible and invincible young adults to realistic, mature parents, learning to cope with their place in the cycle of life, which at some point will include the death of their own parents.

This process is not easy or smooth for anyone. The ongoing journey, even when both natural parents are still married, can often be painful, tumultuous and overwhelming. Don't give up. If you were still living full-time with your first spouse and the children you were raising together, then you would be seeing a good deal of the same behavior. For the most part, your children would probably be acting just like your stepchildren, which means they could be driving you and your new spouse equally crazy.

Your own biological children might be thinking and saying the same bad things about you, your parenting and their other parent, be it your old spouse or the new one. If your biological children are sufficiently comfortable with you, they might even call you the same bad names while pointing out the same shortcomings as your stepchildren.

All children behave this way at times, particularly when stressed. Unlike you, the supposed adult, they haven't yet developed the coping skills that you hopefully possess. Try to be thick-skinned about what they say. It's often not about you, but more about the parenting role you are playing in their life.

As the adult, you are supposed to understand, set limits and not over react when challenged. You are not your children's pal; you are their parent. Being a pal implies a peer relationship that is inappropriate in these circumstances.

The growth and development of everyone's children are usually time limited. And the process of bringing together two groups of people with their own history and way of doing things takes even more time and energy.

Be patient.

"When I was a boy of fourteen," Mark Twain once said, "my father was so ignorant I could hardly stand to have the old man around. But when I got to be twenty-one, I was astonished at how much he had learned."

EMBRACING DIVERSITY UNDER THE SAME ROOF

Children, biological or step, don't necessarily have the same tastes, values, goals, abilities, interests, and ways of doing things that their parents do but for some reason, many parents try to force their children into becoming clones of themselves. This need to control and manipulate is often intended to reassure the parents that their own values are the right ones or because they are genuinely convinced that their way is the only way. Most parent-child power struggles are essentially about the need for control and the natural reaction against it.

First of all, parents must listen to their children and do their best to understand where they are coming from, rather than trying to coerce them into a type of behavior that simply makes sense to the parent but not to the child. Because children introduce parents to new ways of looking at things, if you are open and available to accept them, they will not only keep you young; they can earn you a lot of respect from your new stepchildren.

This is not to say that one should be blindly permissive and tolerant. Common sense should dictate what might be harmful or destructive to your child and what needs to be openly discussed. This is true for biological and stepchildren. It makes no difference. Just as you would with your own children, you must make every effort to understand who your stepchildren are, what is important to them, what they like to do, who their friends are and what they do for fun. And you have to do this in a relatively non-judgmental way, just as you would with your own child.

If your stepchildren like to do things that are different from what you or your own children enjoy that doesn't make them difficult or imply that they have to change. Just because the child's friends are different from those you might have picked, it doesn't necessarily make the child a bad kid or mean he or she has bad friends. All of that simply means that you must get bigger and embrace the diversity!

In the context of a new blended family, the interest that a new adult shows in a child can carry enormous weight. The child and his or her parent will appreciate it and your relationships will grow in very positive ways.

When children reach late adolescence these relationships become tested in ways that you may not have anticipated. I had trouble at times connecting with Andrew as he grew older. Then, unexpectedly, he started keeping me company when I walked the dog at night. We got into some very interesting conversations, which helped me understand him better, and I think he got to see what I was like when we were alone and away from any distractions.

Usually, when you abandon your own biases and try to understand someone, you can find qualities you like in that person and improve your relationship. Conversely, when you focus solely on the negative qualities, those traits may be magnified, not just in your eyes, but also in the other person's, making him or her even more unwilling to change. Once you focus on the negative, your relationship stalls. This is true whether you are dealing with your children, your stepchildren or other people in your life.

Even if a child you are living with and you cannot stand each other, it is mainly up to you as the adult to try and make it all work. Marriage the second time around is a package deal and if you are a serious person you'd better commit to making all of the relationships succeed.

Sometimes, success will show itself in unexpected ways.

I like to collect T-shirts when I travel and enjoy wearing them when I am not working. One fall day, I could not find any of my favorite T-shirts. I looked everywhere, and they simply could not be found. There were too many of them to simply disappear, but eventually I gave up looking.

Then Thanksgiving came and Barry returned from his first semester at college with a large bag of laundry, overflowing with all of my missing T-shirts. I went ballistic, and fortunately Barry was not home at the time.

"How could he take my favorite T-shirts without even saying anything or asking permission?" I asked Donna incredulously. "I've been looking for those things for two months. He has his own dad. If he wants to take someone's T-shirts, why doesn't he take his, and not mine?"

As usual, Donna had a wise answer immediately ready to calm me down.

"He really likes and admires you," she said. "That's why he took them. If he didn't like and respect you, he wouldn't have taken your clothes to wear.'

That made sense, and rather than staying angry, I was flattered that Barry thought my T-shirts were neat, and was actually wearing them.

MEETING YOUR NEW STEPCHILDREN ON THEIR SIDE OF THE MIDDLE

None of us appreciates other people intruding on our life, whether it's to tell us what to do or what we are not doing correctly, particularly when doing something correctly usually means doing it their way. This is even more irksome when they do it on their schedule, rather than ours, or when we did not ask for any input and they provided it anyway.

It should not be surprising then that if you impose yourself on your children, biological or step, they may resent it and let you know about it—by aggressively complaining or by passive-aggressively not doing what you told them to do or doing it slowly. When you intrude at the wrong time, the underlying message is that your children are wrong and what they are doing is not okay, and that you, the adult, will straighten them out, whether they want it or not. That message may only add to a feeling they already have that they are always a little wrong in your eyes, which your criticism, even constructive, can only worsen.

Children will eventually ask for assistance once they realize that they are stuck and know they can ask for help from an available, supportive person who will not rub their nose in what they do not know. It is often better not to jump in and correct them or try to take over by telling your stepchildren what they are doing wrong. Just make yourself available. Let the child know you may have some insight into the problem and that you're willing to help—if asked. Then leave it. It may be hard to watch a child stumble and wait patiently until he or she asks for assistance. Children must get help on their own terms, not yours. When you wait until you are asked rather than inserting yourself into a situation, a child will be much more appreciative and value your input.

Here's more proof that a trained professional is not always the best role model outside the office. One day, Donna and I took the kids out into the country to shoot skeet. If you think about it, it's a rather daunting task to shoot a small clay plate that is rapidly flying away from you when that gun makes a lot of noise and smacks you in the shoulder after you pull the trigger. When it was Barry's turn, he kept missing the target. I jumped in to tell him what he was doing wrong and how to do it right. Classic bonehead. Rather than appreciating my input and thanking me for it, which I thought at the time he might do, he grew increasingly angry. Clearly he was upset that he was missing the targets, but his anger focused more and more on me, and he complained that I was laughing at him and trying to make him miss. It was a no win deal and I eventually shut up.

The next time we went, Barry asked me what he should do to improve his technique. He realized I had some idea of what I was doing and recognized that my help might afford him more success, but he had to solicit my help when he wanted it, and on his terms, not mine.

DEMOCRACY IN ACTION: BLENDING MULTIPLE STRUCTURES UNDER ONE ROOF

We all need structure in life. Even rebellious children need a structure to rebel against. We are born into structure and live within some form of it through most, if not all of our lives. This structure determines our values—as individuals, families and a society.

When two families join together under one roof, each spouse brings his or her own structure, including rules, roles and family rituals. Integrating all of this can be challenging. While there must be some areas of agreement to get to the marrying stage, it also means that both parties must compromise. This is hard enough when there is just one set of kids in the house but it becomes significantly more difficult when two groups of children begin living together. What was once a familiar sense of structure may be compromised. Some negotiating naturally occurs before the wedding, but no one can anticipate what will happen once everyone is living together under everyday conditions.

Working out a style of structure that everyone can live with means that the new set of parents must be clear, consistent and understandable to each other and their children. That includes a precise explanation of what will occur when children do not follow the new rules of the collective house. Children should be informed why they are being disciplined and it should happen as soon as possible after the inciting event. Punishment should be an incentive not to do things but it should also help children learn to avoid behavior that can become more painful later on, particularly outside the family.

When administered correctly and in appropriate doses, discipline and structure can be fair and consistent, and should show our children that what we do matters and that someone cares about them and their behavior.

It is critically important who does the disciplining, particularly with children because they need to feel that the person doing the punishing cares about them, and is not just doing it to assert authority or physical strength.

A single mother newly divorced cannot say to her son, "Wait until your father comes home." She has to do it herself, which is harder because in those situations the child may have also become her confidant. After having been "buddies" it is hard for the parent to instill discipline or change the rules. This is particularly true when you add someone new to the mix and then try to explain why there are new rules and what the consequences are if they are not followed.

Because it is difficult to be fair and consistent after a divorce, parental discipline can often fluctuate, especially considering the added stress of taking care of everything—job, home and children. A single parent can become overly permissive or too strict, either ignoring or overreacting to a child's behavior. If that happens, guilt may cause the punishment to be overturned, which effectively minimizes whatever lesson the children were supposed to learn. Whatever poor behavior the children engaged in gets ignored. Even worse for the single, custodial parent is the fear that the children may say they want to live with the other, less strict parent, who bends to the child's wishes. The fact that a child is growing up in a home without both biological parents causes a great deal of anxiety among single parents. Guilt is always present, and whenever anything does not go well for your child it is very difficult not to feel as if it's your fault.

Non-custodial parents in a divorce can also have trouble disciplining the children. They often worry or feel guilty that if they come down too hard on their child, the child won't like them or want to visit them again. This guilt is multiplied for the post-divorce parent who can't stop thinking that if they had done something differently they would still be together as an intact family.

Any version of this can lead to shortchanging your children. When everyone does not participate in setting rules—and enforcing them—your children may feel hurt, neglected and angry. Some children act out their feelings with negative behavior like running away, doing poorly in school, using drugs or hanging around with other children who also feel neglected emotionally.

After Donna and I had been together for a short time, Barry began a new school and was not doing well. Donna and his father talked to him about it, but nothing changed. The school's policy was to send notes home right away about problems, which meant that Donna hated opening the mail for fear of finding out again that Barry was either not prepared for class, had not handed in homework or had done badly on a test. When Barry realized these notes were coming home, he got upset and thought that the whole thing must've been my idea, that this sort of thing never happened before his parents' divorce and I came into the picture. Regardless, for some reason within a short time, Barry's grades and behavior improved dramatically, but not without some initial clashes.

Developing new rules and discipline in blended families takes time, tolerance, and the process clearly works better when everyone is included. Inclusion means that everyone's input including the children's should be heard, even if the end result is not quite, or anywhere near what they wanted. General guidelines and rules are easy to work out because you have probably been living with them for a time, but moving on to specifics, or trying to develop rules as issues come up is harder. That is why it is important for everyone to sit down after a moment of crisis and develop strategies for discipline. The earlier it is done, the better it will be for everyone.

When a new spouse joins a family that has had fluctuating discipline, is somewhat structure-less or has a guilt-ridden parent, it may be tempting for the new person to jump in and take over, trying to save everybody immediately. That can cause the biological parent to either withdraw by passively supporting the new spouse or jump in to defend the children. When a biological parent withdraws, the children resent it and their behavior often gets worse.

A relative outsider can't effectively discipline someone else's children unless this person has a relationship with the parent and the children. If the parent or children do not think that the discipliner also cares about them, the situation can escalate. The parent sympathizes with and attempts to protect the children from the stepparent, which causes problems to arise. It antagonizes the stepparent who feels that he or she has no input, and may threaten the future relationships. It ignores the reality that the children may have done something wrong and that their behavior merits a response with consequences.

When a parent reflexively bonds with the children by always taking their side, it lets them think they are running the show, and that nothing they do will have any significant consequences for them. This kind of behavior often then leads to the parent overreacting, which makes things even worse. That is why escalating levels of discipline really work better than ignoring and then overreacting to punish the child with both barrels.

Even worse, threatening a child to go live with the other parent if they don't do what you tell them gives the impression that your child is unloved, unlovable and expendable, or loved only on a conditional basis, which further adds to the fear of being abandoned again. Children do better when they can flow back and forth between their biological parents, particularly after the divorce. If possible, some effort should be made to have similar rules and consequences at both places, which helps to eliminate the playing off of one parent against the other.

Trying to work out an understanding of all of the rules, and the discipline, as much as you can from the beginning, helps keep everyone from losing control, overreacting, and later regretting what they did.

Try to establish the same rules for your children and your stepchildren when they are living under your roof. Work out with your new spouse a new set of Dos and Don'ts. Because the same situations seem to always reappear, anticipating them ahead of time helps everyone.

Children almost always think that their stepparent will be harder on them than their own parent is. When the biological parent actually does favor their own children though, their kids feel entitled, as if regular rules do not apply to them. The stepchildren feel abused, like the ones in fairy tales, which makes it much more difficult for the new family to bond. The children may then not want to come to visit their biological parent in their stepparent's home, further adding to the children's feeling that they have no place of their own, and that their own parent allows this new person to pick on them, which makes their situation even more depressing.

Treating your children and your stepchildren differently is destructive to the relationship between the new couple, and makes the lives of the children more difficult. It becomes an ongoing source of conflict between the adults, and is another factor that can cause a new couple to split up rather than to try to work out their differences.

After you have remarried and your biological children come to visit, they need to know about any new rules, particularly if they were not involved in helping to set them up. This should start on the initial visit by explaining simply the rules in the new house and your new spouse's preferences. It is worth pointing out again, that while you may have tolerated certain things in the past, such behavior may not be acceptable now that more people are involved and living together. Going over these things in the beginning and reviewing them on a regular basis will often save everyone a lot of time, grief, misunderstandings and hurt feelings. Oh yes, and screaming!

This will help everyone feel they are part of the same team effort. If only I had known this better when I first remarried. At that time, I never really sat down with Frank to tell him that things were going to be a little different, to explain what Donna was like and what the new rules would be. I was so glad to see him that I let him do everything just as he had before.

Donna resented that for a while. She felt like I wasn't supporting her efforts to get everything to run smoothly, and felt that she was constantly fighting with everyone. It must have seemed like all I wanted was to have everyone happy while I spent time with Frank. Maybe that's true, but giving Donna a Mary Poppins complex was not exactly the right idea.

When you jump into raising two sets of children with what feels like limited resources of time, money, energy and emotion, it is hard to treat your stepchildren as you do your biological children. This may be exacerbated by having limited time or access to your natural children, and wanting them to have a good time with you so they will like you and want to come back. With your stepchildren living with you on an ongoing basis, you may feel that you don't have to treat them in the same way because they are there all the time or they are not really yours. But stop right there. Your whole family will quickly realize your mistake and will react accordingly when you treat your natural children and your stepchildren differently. All the kids will notice and talk about the way some of them are treated differently than others. This means that as hard as it may be, everything will go easier for everyone if you can treat everyone the same—from the beginning.

At one point, Donna would get on Frank about not cleaning up after snacking at night with his friends. Barry and Susan finally said something to her about how unfair she was being because when they did the same thing occasionally she didn't seem to get upset. Donna apologized to Frank and it soon became a non-issue. Once again, kids to the rescue of their parents!

The decision about when, how, and what to discipline your child for is a very difficult one that only you, their parent, can really make. In theory, you have been doing it for some time before your new spouse entered the picture, and you are the one who knows their history, as well as what was done in the past. You are also the one who has the relationship with them, and you are the one they know cares about them. Often when children act out, they want a response from you—just you—and their behavior may be driven by trying to get that reaction out of you. If you ignore them or delegate it to someone else, they miss out on whatever it is they want, and their behavior will often escalate until you do respond.

While you may want to use the stepparent's input you need to be the actual disciplinarian. Your new spouse may be helpful in pointing out things that you miss, ignore, or have let slide in the past, but only you know if there is a reason why you choose to let something go.

Early on in my new marriage, I would get enormously upset at something Barry would do, something I did not like that he knew would upset me. I felt he often just wanted to provoke me and after a while I realized that if I told him to stop he would not only continue, but it would culminate into a long argument that always came to the same conclusion.

"You're not my father, who are you to tell me what to do?"

I was not sure that Donna knew what was going on or how I felt about it. Our resolution was for me to tell her what it was that upset me. She would later talk to him and try to get him to change or do what she knew I wanted him to do. Amazingly, it seemed to work most of the time, although usually not in the time frame I would have wanted. In reality though, it happened when it was supposed to.

As a result of that experience and hearing about many others in my practice, I have come to the conclusion that the biological parents are the only ones who can discipline their own children. They know the child's history and how discipline was taken care of in the past. They need to respect the stepparent because they are living with that person, but that person can't be the one to do the disciplining without creating more problems for everyone.

CHAPTER 8

WHO'S ZOOMING WHO?

Maintaining fair and consistent rules (and punishment) is an ongoing source of conflict in every family—divorced or not—which is compounded by children playing one parent off against the other to get what they want. This can occur equally under one roof or through commuting from one household to another.

There are multiple reasons why we may favor one of our own children over others. They may remind us of ourselves, in a good or bad way. We may envy them for being able to do the things we could not or we may struggle over things they can't do but we think they should be able to do, particularly as they are our child. For instance, it's often difficult for college educated parents to deal with a child who has a learning disability, just like it is difficult for a parent who was athletic to have an unathletic child, or an attractive, feminine mom to have a daughter who is a tomboy.

We may even feel that we have to favor a child if a biological parent has been neglectful or if we want one child, who lives with our ex, to have a good time during visits with us. In turn, we could feel as though that relationship could be jeopardized by strict discipline. With any of these examples, the end result is not good, especially when parents favor one child over another—for any reason. Just as a child may play one parent off against another, so can parents use their children to achieve something they think is preferable, when in the end, it will only harm everyone.

SPLITTING: WHEN KIDS PIT PARENTS AGAINST EACH OTHER

The psychological process of playing one parent off against the other is called "splitting" and usually occurs when parents disagree about something. As a result, the child will not learn the proper lesson, and will be falsely led to believe that manipulation is the way to get what you want. When parents can't agree on the importance of a rule or what the consequence of breaking it should be, their other children suffer, too. They notice if one child gets punished more and will play parents off against each other if they see a way to avoid the consequences of bad behavior. When this happens, one child ultimately becomes the scapegoat—the bad kid— while another is seen as the favored child who can do no wrong. Meanwhile, the other children either remain quiet to avoid becoming the scapegoat or do what they want because they feel like they may be criticized anyway and will never be the favored child. Unfortunately, once these family stereotypes of the good and bad kid are formed, it is very difficult for any of the children to change them at home, and even worse they often carry them outside the family into their later life.

When a stepparent enters into the picture, the issue of splitting becomes more complex. The stepparent may buy into the family stereotype of which child is good and which is bad, which unfairly starts the new family off on the wrong foot. When it comes to disciplining, the biological parent tends to become more protective of his or her own children and more critical of the new spouse's. This is a set up for conflict and puts the new couple's relationship at risk.

Confusion is inevitable for children in a blended family if parent-child communication is inconsistent and discipline is arbitrary or unfair.

"When I was little, I thought that the reason my father punished me more severely for things that the other kids got away with was because I was the oldest," a patient once told me. "It was only when I got older that I realized I was not my father's real child, and that my mother had had me with someone else before they got married. Then, I understood why he treated me that way, and it was terrible. I am still almost as mad at my mother for not sticking up for me as I am at him doing what he did. But it also made me stronger and more successful. None of my brothers and sisters was there for me when we were growing up but now they all come to me for help and money. Today, I work hard to protect my kids whenever my husband seems to be too strict or unfair." When our two youngest boys were little, they would always ask Donna and me which one was our favorite. When each of them was alone with me, I would tell him that he was my favorite. One day, when they were about seven and eight years old, after they had been whispering together at the table, they made an announcement.

"You said I was your favorite," one began.

"Which one of us really is?" the other chimed in.

I was caught, but I told them that they were both my favorites and that ended the discussion forever. Lucky me. I don't suspect my feet (in my mouth) would have tasted too good.

REDEFINING DISCIPLINE

"What do you think you're doing?"

"Who do you think you are?"

"You can't tell me what to do, or make me do anything."

"You're not my (father or mother) so I don't have to listen to you."

It can be frustrating at times to realize that you are living in a household with someone else's children, who may be out of control or behave disrespectfully to their biological parent. Then when you become involved and try to assert reason or discipline, the child may lose control even more simply because you jumped in. You thought you were helping but the point you were making, or the behavior you were trying to fix, often gets lost in that process. You become the bad guy, the child learns nothing, and your new spouse may feel that you just don't understand. It is frustrating and can leave you feeling powerless.

It takes longer and is much less direct to communicate your wishes through your spouse but that is the best approach when you are unhappy with a situation and think the child needs discipline. If you don't like the child's behavior, tell your spouse. Explain what you don't like, allow your spouse to respond, and discipline the child, if required. If you don't think discipline is being handled properly by the parent, speak up. You can provide support and play a complementary role in areas where the parent may have trouble; disciplining children often is difficult, especially for single parents dealing with latent guilt over a divorce.

In my personal experience, even after many years, and at a point when we consider all the children to be ours, this approach still seems to work much better than jumping in and disciplining, or even advising your stepchild directly.

Once there is a level of trust, you can say what you think, but that is best done in a mentoring or coaching manner rather than in the role of the child's primary disciplinarian.

ROLE MODELING

"Give a man a fish and he will eat for a day; teach him to fish and he will eat for a lifetime."

In order to survive in the real world, children need to be taught life skills. That is part of the reason why childhood and adolescence take so long. Becoming a functioning adult is not easy! These skills are all best learned in a positive, supportive setting where mistakes can be made, where consequences are not catastrophic and where help is available when we get stuck. This is as true in a family with two biological parents as in a single parent family or in a blended one. Minimizing stress at home is important, and a parent, teacher, surrogate, mentor or coach can play a role in teaching a child how to live. Who does the teaching just depends on what needs to be taught, who is available, the child's age, and who follows through. It is important to help our children by supporting authority figures, but sometimes you have to reach outside your usual network to get help. That can be a tutor, coach, a relative or even a therapist, as long as it is someone who cares about the child and knows something about the issue.

Role modeling is unconscious learning by watching, seeing, doing, and trying to emulate without verbal instruction, rather unlike the old adage, "Do as I say, not as I do." We all often role model our favorite people. This is very different than teaching, which is conscious, planned, and verbal. Role modeling is similar to imprinting in baby animals that will follow whatever they see at a particular moment in their development. This process continues well past childhood and is why many of us have mentors or people we grew up with that we still admire.

If you observe young children walking next to a parent, you will notice that they often hold their body up and walk in the same fashion as the parent. They will also have many of the same mannerisms. Not only do children model their parent's physical behaviors, but they also emulate their values, interests, and the coping mechanisms. Children's interactions with their parents, and their observations of their parents' interaction with each other also serve as the primary model for interacting with others.

How many times have each of us found that we are doing things our parents did, or treating our children in ways that we said we would never do when we had children of our own? This includes the people I see in my practice who not only have drug and alcohol problems, but also had parents who were the same way. They swore as children that when they grew up, they would never be like their own parents, but they are in fact behaving the same way.

"I can't believe that it's happening to me. I am doing the same stuff to my kids, and saying the same thing to them that my parents used to say to me that used to drive me crazy, things that I swore I would never do as a parent."

It is natural to feel hurt, sad, or angry about things that happen to you, especially during and after a divorce, but teaching children to label those feelings, talk about them, and learn to use them effectively is something that parents can teach even before preschool. In turn, it helps children to realize that they do not need to avoid feelings or act them out by hitting, yelling, sulking, running away or doing chemicals to deal or avoid dealing with them.

What this means is that people are usually successful in their interactions with others to the extent that they understand their own feelings, and then control their actions in response to those feelings. This means that you, your children, and your new spouse should set up an atmosphere where feelings can be acknowledged, talked about and understood. No matter how painful the situation and the feelings may be, everyone is on the way to things improving.

The benefits of good parenting have been well illustrated by a patient of mine.

"I really think of my stepfather as my real dad. He was always there for me. He came to all my sports events and helped me play ball when I was growing up. He had been a pilot and was my role model and inspiration. That's why I am a pilot today. I always knew I had a dad. I even saw a fair amount of him. But my stepdad was really a great person."

When Donna and I traveled together to California to visit Frank, we often went out for dinner and shopping. He always said, "Dad, I like it now that Donna is with us because she picks better places to eat," Frank preferred shopping with Donna, too because in his words, "She has much better taste than you do, Dad, and she knows what goes with what."

Initially, children learn most everything from their parents, but by the time they begin school they already have some idea from the media about what is going on in the world. While their first role models are their biological parents and other relatives, introducing a stepparent into the mix provides a whole new world of ideas and examples of how people behave and interact. Hopefully, your child will gain a great deal by observing the interaction of their new stepparent with their biological parent.

Children learn just by being in different settings, observing table manners, what clothes people wear and how they socialize. It is important to let children observe first and become comfortable with a new stepparent as a positive force.

Donna couldn't believe it when we first got together and she discovered an expired ketchup bottle on my kitchen counter. It was no wonder. I only cooked occasionally, mostly in the summer, and especially for Frank. With Donna in the picture, just being herself, he became excited about going to the supermarket to get the stuff he liked, not to mention having regular meals at home at regular times with her children—just like families do. Frank really enjoyed it and Donna couldn't quite believe that we had been living like a couple of bachelors.

CHAPTER 9

GROWING PAINS

Life as a stepparent can run the gamut from best experience of your life to one of the worst, and quite often it provides both. At times, you may feel that everything you do is wrong and that everyone seems unhappy and considers it your fault. At other times, the pleasures and joys are greater than you could imagine. You may even feel like you have more rewarding interactions with your stepchildren than with your own. But living with someone else's children when you cannot be with your own can seem terribly unfair and downright painful. Knowing that while you are with your stepchildren, your own child is with your ex and his or her significant other is an ongoing hurt that seems as if it will never go away. Hopefully, all the pain and heartache will dissipate and seem worthwhile, especially the first time a stepchild unthinkingly calls you Mom or Dad, or asks to do something together.

YOU'VE MARRIED A FAMILY

Many people pay lip service to the concept of marrying a family, believing they are just marrying the person they dated and fell in love with. This blindly romantic notion is delusional, an effort to continue acting as if you are still in a dating relationship, with the children as an afterthought or as something to merely fit in between career and love life. It implies that your new partner has nothing to do except to work and cater to you, which is unrealistic. Your efforts to continue this fantasy will sooner or later break down because you have married a total package, not just the person of your dreams.

Have you ever heard the phrase "Buyer Beware" when it comes to buying a new couch? It may seem comfortable in the department store but when you get it home it just doesn't feel right and the return policy is not what you thought.

In a second marriage, that package often includes children, an ex-spouse, in-laws (a new set) and some weird relatives. So when you start out with a new blended marriage, how do you enter another person's family and even hope to make a seamless transition?

Separation and loss can turn people inward. They try to reconnect to items and people they felt close to and could depend on in the past. It should not surprise you that the person you have fallen in love with and recently married will continue to be very involved with his or her biological children, even ones that are adult. The kids may have seemed less important while you were dating, but the children are still central to a parent's life.

This means that many of the struggles the two of you have will be about children, not about in-laws, as it may have been in your first marriage. It also means that if you do not like one or all of your new spouse's children before you start out, unless you are willing to change, it will probably get worse, not better. Acceptance is everything, and that applies to more than your new spouse. Your love for this person does not guarantee that you will be crazy about the children.

What about tolerating bad habits, behaviors you do not approve of, ways you think they are spoiled or values that are different than yours or your own kids'? It can be even be worse if you don't approve of something and your new spouse doesn't agree. Biological parents who are still together often can't wait for their own, natural children to pass through adolescence and leave home, so how can you, a stepparent, endure that same adolescent turmoil with someone else's children?

Becoming a new stepparent can seem so daunting, especially if you feel as if you have very little input or control with a child, one who keeps saying, "You can't tell me what to do. You're not my mom or dad."

In first marriages, many people say their problems began when they had children and their spouse became more interested in the children than in their adult relationship. This sense of distance from the new spouse may occur more rapidly in a second marriage when there are already children present. As soon as the knot is tied, the courtship ends, and everyone reverts back to focusing on their own children.

Unless this situation is properly addressed, second marriages won't work. One spouse winds up saying, "I really liked them, but I just couldn't live with their kids because they always put them first."

There is no sure way to navigate this process successfully, but I have discovered some things that worked for me and other couples. First of all, use patience. Blending a family is a long, complex process. Time must be measured in months and years, not days or weeks, and progress occurs slowly. There is never a total reversal or an instantaneous acceptance of the stepparent as the child's savior, newest best friend, or replacement mom or dad. To the extent you recognize that, and look for small positives rather than major shifts, you, your new spouse and your new stepchildren will all benefit.

In my case, nothing prepared me for living full-time with an entirely new family. The struggles began immediately. It was frustrating when Donna's kids pointed out that I wasn't their parent when I tried to tell them to do something. That was often just a symptom of adolescence, but at the time I personalized it because I was the stepparent and feeling vulnerable. It was equally painful—and I can almost still feel the emptiness in the pit of my stomach—to be off doing something with them that was fun and wishing my own child was there to share the experience.

No one can adequately describe the pains and hurt of being a stepparent any more than one can describe the joy. The meaningfulness of attending the school graduation of a stepchild or walking down the aisle with a stepdaughter and hearing her thank you for helping her achieve that milestone is beyond my ability to articulate, but just knowing that I really did have some small part in making it happen is enormously special and I would not trade the experience for anything.

EXPANDING YOUR VOWS

Committing to a new relationship means meeting the challenges and obligations of your new family's day-to-day life. Whether it's "your children," "your spouse's children," or "our children," each of them have activities that merit support from all parents and siblings. In my professional experience, when children participate in an extracurricular activity they like and can begin to excel in, one that ultimately builds self-esteem, they do better in life and are less likely to get into trouble. They don't have to shine like an afternoon TV special, but they do need to know that they have your support and encouragement. It is important to support all of your children by setting aside time to attend activities.

The message you give children if you don't go is that you don't really care about them or what they do, and the message you give your new spouse if you don't participate in his or her children's activities is that you don't really care about something that is very important to him or her. The statement that it makes about you is that you never really bought into the blended family concept, and were just there for your own convenience or just for your spouse. In any case, everyone loses if you follow that path.

The more you engage as a parent the more you will feel a part of everyone's life. Your blended family will feel that you are truly involved with them and they will include you, as well. The emotional pleasure you receive from watching someone you are involved with grow and improve will make it all worthwhile.

Donna used to drive Frank to his football training for what seemed to be every day all summer. It was really a hassle at times because she was working, had our new babies and her own two kids, but it made Frank happy, and he in turn would help Barry and the other kids at home. Me? I sat through Barry and Susan's piano recitals. Today, none of the kids are doing any of those things, but I think it helped us all connect and appreciate each other.

When Barry was little, he was in several soccer leagues and we would drive all over the county to watch him play. I often wondered why I let myself be dragged along, when I could have been doing any number of things I thought I preferred. But I always enjoyed watching Barry play soccer and I felt proud whenever anyone acknowledged my involvement.

Years later, Barry would go to his little brothers' activities when we could not. He would take them out after the games and do things together, just as I had done with him. When

I mentioned to Donna how pleased I was about that, and what a good job he was doing as a big brother, she said, "Well it's because he learned that from you. You were a good role model."

At least I got it right some of the time.

INCLUSION VS. INTRUSION

It is relatively easy in a first marriage to decide who to include in special events, because in the beginning it usually means everyone is welcome, including both sets of parents, other relatives, and old family friends—until people drop out by not participating, being negative or moving away. Ultimately, a married couple develops their own network as they add new friends, their children's friends and even their children's friends' parents.

In a second marriage, particularly at first, it may seem unclear who should be part of this new blended family. Close relatives of each spouse are relatively easy to include, as are people who have previously been a significant part of either spouse's and children's lives.

There is often a temptation to exclude the ex-spouse and his or her family, including the grandparents and other relatives, because they may have taken sides in the divorce. From the children's perspective, these people have been part of their life from the onset and should continue to be involved in the future. Therefore, they should be involved in major activities. Not to include the other parent at a child's birthday party or an event at school is a guarantee that problems will arise, even if the other parent chooses not to attend after being informed. One parent choosing not to attend may be that parent's own problem, but it is also something the child will have to deal with. But not extending an invitation is simply close-minded and offers no favor to your child.

Children do better when everyone is included. It reassures them that they will not be abandoned again and reinforces the significance they hold to others. Involving everyone in special events also supports the notion that life goes on despite the changes. An open door also acknowledges that there will be significant events that are meant for everyone to share in the future. You may as well begin positively by taking the high road on those occasions where everyone can be included, such as school events, graduations, birthday parties, concerts and sports. However you slice it, inclusion is in your children's best interest.

Inclusion also means remaining consistent and involved, so that stepchildren will come to see you as a resource and not just their natural parent's friend or spouse. You may eventually start thinking of them as your children, and have the same hopes, aspirations and fears that you have for your own children.

When children see that their stepparent is dependable, predictable and there for the long haul they can feel secure, confident and strong. It is very scary for anyone, but particularly for a child to be around someone who seems unpredictable, and will overreact one day, ignore things the next day, and then respond appropriately the third day. The best way to build trust is to let your stepchildren feel as though you are there for them, and not that you despise them or that they are a burden to you. It makes a big difference if you try to get to know them, and get involved in the things that are important to them. Again, it is not necessary to thrust yourself into the middle of everything they do, or try to be a super-parent in an effort to get them to like you or make up for the inadequacies of their absent biological parent. It is enough to be there, get involved with them, not ignore them, and not allow yourself to be run off by them when they are less than happy and try to make your life difficult.

In turn, your stepchildren will want to get to know you and what is important to you. They may ask about you if you are open and available to them, but if they do not, you can volunteer information about yourself, your interests, and your own experience. As this happens you may find yourself developing a more meaningful and deeper relationship with them, and may even get to the point where you genuinely like them more than you ever thought you could. They, in turn, will get to like you more, may want to spend more time with you and do more things with you. When that begins to happen you realize that all your efforts have been worthwhile, and that everyone, but particularly you, has benefited. Your new spouse will be pleased and appreciative of your efforts, and may even become closer to you. Even the ex will appreciate your efforts to help and will be grateful that you genuinely care about his or her child, and may in turn feel less pressure to fight with everyone, while needing to provide additional emotional and financial support. As time progresses, you may also develop a friend in the child who may like to do things with you, often some of the things they learned from you.

The secret is simple: time, commitment and consistency. Those three gifts will present the most ironic surprises.

After seven years of us living together and struggling through a good deal of it, Barry was ready to go off to college. There had been times over the years when I felt like I was marking the days off on a calendar, but just before Barry left we really got to enjoy each other. We became real friends, and I missed him dearly when he left. I know that it all had to do with my being there, committed and steady, for my son.

LESSONS LEARNED

1. You are not your children's pal; you are their parent.

2. Be open and available to accept your new stepchildren.

3. Make every effort to understand your stepchild.

4. Commit to making all relationships succeed.

5. Children must get help on their own terms, not yours.

6. Parents must be clear, consistent and understandable to each other and their children.

7. Both parents must participate in setting rules—and enforcing them.

8. Develop joint strategies for discipline.

9. Establish the same rules for your children and your stepchildren.

10. Biological parents are the only ones who can discipline their own children.

BECOMING THE BEST STEPPARENT YOU CAN BE

CHAPTER 10

WHOSE SIDE ARE YOU ON?

Whether you are a single parent or part of a blended family, if you are a biological parent you are responsible for raising your own children. This is true in the eyes of every Family Court, in the view of your ex-spouse, your children's school and most other facets of modern society. You can rationalize all you want, but your child is your child. Whatever ideas, suggestions and critiques you may hear from relatives or your new spouse, the buck starts and stops with you. YOU. You can look around all you want for whatever bailout you think may exist, but rest assured, there is no alternative. If you have children, step up to the plate and do the right thing. Frankly, if your marriage doesn't work out, the kids will still be your responsibility.

Most of us have grown up in some sort of a family, and that experience influences how we view what a family should be, how we behave when we become parents and our expectations of how our spouse should act. That is why we frequently find ourselves saying, "I can't believe I'm acting like my father or mother, doing the same stuff I hated as a kid, and here I am doing it to my kids all over again."

While you think you may be repeating what you always saw as your parents' mistakes, history shows us that parental roles are always changing. Gender politics, the job market and traditional mores all play a role in influencing our idea of what an ideal parenting situation may be. But anyone who has lived through a divorce realizes that any attempt to automatically graft the old style of parental functions onto a single parent or blended family doesn't necessarily work. In today's world, if it's working, keep it up!

REDEFINING PARENTAL RESPONSIBILITY

Following a divorce, a single parent must fill both parental roles, including caretaking, meal preparation and chauffeuring, just to name a few. When your involvement with someone else leads to a new marriage, you open the door to an entirely new set of responsibilities. They may resemble very little of your previous married life. Your new spouse is probably different than your first, to say the least. His or her children are individuals in their own right. Taken together, you have a new family to learn about, with their own ways of doing things. The children are used to things being done a certain way, by both parents or just one, and you, as a new person in their life, can't possibly know the ins and outs of how they've lived. Personalities are not interchangeable and your new spouse and children will have their own ideas and experiences about parenting and family life. Because of that, if you try and recreate things exactly as they were in your previous household with your own children, you're probably guaranteed to fail. Imagine if your new family sends you grocery shopping with their list of what to get and you decide on your own to buy other things that are the wrong brand, size and flavor. Everyone will be unhappy and you will soon be returning to the store to atone for your sins.

All of this new parental responsibility will be overwhelming if you try and jump in as if you know it all. Conversely, if your new spouse is abruptly thrust into a position of responsibility for your children, you are setting up a situation that cannot reasonably succeed. They can't ever do everything as well as you, in good part because they don't have your experience with what happened before, and they don't have the trust and support of your children.

More importantly, a child who is suddenly told that someone they barely know will be suddenly instrumental in managing their life may become very upset and rebel, either actively or passively, which could drive your new spouse away instead of them becoming more involved and supportive.

One of my patients, struggling herself as a parent in a blended family, put it this way: "I really do not know what I should or could do. My new husband says that I am too indulgent and spoil my son, who he thinks needs to have discipline and consequences for everything he does. But my new husband is also a retired military guy so everything with him is rigid and by the book. My son does need some structure, but he really doesn't do well with the kind of rigid controls my husband is trying to put on him. He's a teenager and he doesn't like being told what to do. He says he hates my new husband.

"I just don't know what to do. I feel like I have to choose between them, that I can't win, and that I may lose one of them. He is my son, though. His father really was never there for him, I had to make it up to him, and I am all he has. I really wanted him to have a more positive role model, but this may be too much."

Marriage, be it your first or last, is a trial and error process. Same with parenting. The most you can hope for is to not make the same mistake twice.

WHEN YOUR SPOUSE'S CHILDREN COME FIRST

A divorce will cause disappointment, loss, anguish and hurt in anyone, but for a child it is more traumatic than almost anything else except the death or catastrophic illness of a parent. Since children usually have not yet developed sufficient coping skills, their emotions may often turn to anger and sometimes rage. Unfortunately, these negative reactions, stemming in large part from a sense of powerlessness, may never be totally resolved. Children can remain hypersensitive to a variety of minor things for many years. While their response to current situations will stir up bad memories of past hurts and frustrations, it often has nothing specific to do with you, but rather with what you represent as a stepparent. But once you're in the picture, you can become a lightning rod for their feelings. This is more common when you are new in the relationship. Most likely, it will improve over time if you hang in there, tolerate what feels like abuse, and help everyone move through it. The positive thing to remember is that even when you are getting the brunt of a child's bad reaction simply because you are there, it can also be a result of the child feeling safe enough with you to vent their feelings.

If your stepchildren feel that they have been wronged, they may not feel safe blowing up at the supposed offending biological parent for fear that they will anger the parent and then have to face even worse consequences. When you are the focus of the child's rage about an event like that, try to recognize it, accept it for the moment, and try not to escalate it. Remember, their anger is often not about you. This is not the time to point out to your stepchildren that you are innocent and that it's really their biological parent who they're angry at. That only fuels the fire and puts you at risk of becoming an even bigger bad guy.

Hopefully, your stepchildren will eventually appreciate your patience and best efforts. As they get older, they might be able to discriminate between you, as their stepparent, and the biological parent who hurt them, but that awareness and insight is unlikely to occur during the moment of conflict.

Whenever Barry's dad broke his promise at the last minute to come by and pick up his son to do something, Barry would feel hurt and become extremely angry. If I happened to be the one around the house, his anger—real or imagined—would focus squarely on me.

Occasionally I would say something like, "I know you're really mad at your dad because he disappointed you. You're hurt and angry, and that's why you're taking it out on me."

Ouch! Wrong thing to say. How did I ever pass Psychology 101?

Barry's response was usually quite direct.

"You're a butt, George. Don't use that psychiatry crap on me. I am mad at you because you're a butt; it's got nothing to do with anything else."

As you both start over, remember that your new spouse has been a parent to your stepchildren for a long time, and will continue that role for the duration of all your lives. It is quite possible that your respective parenting strategies were a reason why you were both drawn to each other. That means you cannot get in the middle of the relationship your new spouse and your stepchildren have already built together, nor can you ask your spouse to reshuffle his or her own priorities to make yourself more important. It's a futile effort, and your spouse will ultimately resent you for it.

In the aftermath of a divorce, parents often feel guilty about breaking up the child's original biological family. When children are struggling with transitions, they need their parents that much more. Even when parents cannot really do anything to improve the situation, they often feel like they are the best person to be involved. This means you need to be supportive and understanding of your new spouse's choices, even if it means less adult time together. There is no way that you can demand attention during these circumstances.

The worst dilemma for parents is to feel they must choose between a child and a spouse. This conundrum is heightened when the spouse is new, the child is needy, and the parent feels guilty. This happens in all newly joined families. While it's important that time be made for you and your new relationship, it is unrealistic to think your spouse can serve both relationships at the same time. Do not make the person you profess to love and care for feel obligated to choose between you and a child. Just be supportive and wait your turn. It should come.

If you feel that in every instance when the two of you are about to spend time together the child precipitates a crisis, pulling his or her biological parent into the middle, you should be able to point that out to your spouse. Be sure though to note that this has been a pattern over time before you jump in, and then make time to discuss the issue and then see if the two of you can't work out a better way to deal with the attention-seeking child.

When Donna and I got married, I soon realized that when the telephone rang, no matter what we might be talking about, if it was one of the children—whoever's children—everything else was put on hold and the first order of business was to deal with the child. That is as true when they are twenty-two years old or two. It's like a fire drill. When the bell goes off, you take care of business, no questions asked.

It boils down to a matter of trust. Children need to learn to trust you as a new parental figure and that simply takes time. Look for little signs of progress, not for immediate, major, and dramatic changes. Recognize that your expectations may be much higher than they should be and that you may be looking for progress to occur sooner than what is realistic.

Whatever issues a child may have, don't give up on them, and don't let your spouse, either. Children may not respond on your first, second or even third approach, but keep at it and always keep the door open. Keep working in non-threatening ways to stay in contact and try to maintain upbeat but honest communication. Let their biological parent help the process. Children usually want the connection as much or more than you do, although they may not be able to tell you that initially, or for a significant period of time, after the new marriage.

When the relationship between you and the stepchild begins to improve, which it almost certainly will, you will feel that it has been well worth the effort, even if it took years, not months. As a clinician, it pains me to hear again and again from patients who finally began to get close to their own parent right before their parent's death that they wished they had started that process much sooner.

Think of it this way: you love your new spouse unconditionally, right? Well, why not take the same approach with the children?

BECOMING A FRIEND AND MENTOR

When children feel anxious, uncertain and somewhat lost in their new family situation, they may set up situations to test you as well as find out where they fit in. Whose side are you on? If you play that game, someone will feel like the loser, and that just can't happen. Everyone wants to feel special and important, and these little tests are often a way to try and see who is more important to you. Real love has no favorites, and that's all you really need to remember.

At other times you are asked to decide about a situation, but you clearly can't be a real judge because you weren't there or don't have all the facts, and by the time you are called in to intervene, the facts you get are already mixed up with everyone's feelings. Try not to be a knee-jerk responder, who always takes the side of one person or the other. If you always support your new spouse and assume your children are always wrong and just causing trouble, they will feel as though they are bad, resent the stepparent, think that you don't care about them, and your actions will keep the two of them from ever developing a healthy relationship. If you always assume that your child is right and the spouse is at fault, you run the risk of making your spouse feel unimportant and create a situation where there is never genuine fairness and where no problem will ever have a satisfactory resolution.

When Barry would get mad about something, I would usually tell him to chill because he was setting a bad example for our younger kids. That just made him escalate his behavior in front of them, which made me madder. Ultimately, Donna would jump in and help Barry resolve whatever was bothering him. This included telling him that he did need to be a role model for the little kids and that he had to respect me. Later, she would tell me not to provoke him, but she also took my hand and told me that I was right, but that Barry was going through a rough time. It was a tough balancing act for her.

Your children need to know you understand some of what they are going through, and that you will give them the benefit of the doubt when issues arise. Be supportive, even when you know they are wrong, which you can tell them after the heat of the moment has passed. If you are not on their side at least some of the time, who will be?

The first summer Donna and I and our children were all together, we decided to send the two older children together to a two-week camp. As we were getting the car packed up, Frank said he wanted to take his weight lifting set with him. Donna thought that was silly, but it seemed to be important to Frank, so I agreed that he could. I really thought it was a little over the top, and I certainly felt stupid carrying a set of weights and a weight bench up two flights of stairs in a dormitory for a high school kid, but lifting weights to get ready for fall football was a big part of his identity and it was important for him. Looking back, sore back and all, I believe I did the right thing. Yes, even me, and all because I put my children first.

CHAPTER 11

MANAGING RELATIONSHIPS

Finding new love and starting over with a new family means apprehensions about finding someone, integrating your children and theirs, and having more children together. Hopefully, as this process unfolds, your children will settle down and become happy and comfortable in a new situation.

Then again, everything will not run smoothly all the time. Invariably, something will happen to stir up the pot, whether it's a glitch with your spouse or another round of testing by the children. Just because things have been going well, or the children are older, does not mean that they don't still feel the need for extra attention. Take a step back and give them the benefit of the doubt before you jump in. These situations can be an opportunity for you and the stepparent to co-parent. The stepparent is likely more removed from the situation and will be able to help you understand what is driving your biological child's actions. The stepparent can and should be a resource for you, especially if he or she is not as sensitive to the child's behavior. This may even allow you, the natural parent, to take a proverbial deep breath, stop reacting, and see what is going on, which is often not so terrible.

Don't forget that if your children are having a hard time, you should be the one to try to understand why and help them out of it. Because you might be over-eager to have your children and your new spouse get along you may jump on the children because they are not making that getting along any easier, or are embarrassing you when you know they could act better. Give them a break. You are the one who can help them manage the situation.

One day, Barry brought home a report card that was less than glowing. Donna expressed her displeasure.

"What happened? I expect more than this from you. There is no reason you shouldn't or couldn't do better."

"I can't help it Mom, I have a lot of stress in my life."

"Stress? What kind of stress can you have in your life? You are twelve years old."

"Look, I was the youngest kid, the youngest boy and the youngest grandchild in my whole family," Barry explained. "My parents said they'd never get a divorce. Then we moved and they got a divorce. Then my mom gets married and there's this new man I'm living with, and I have a stepbrother who comes with him and lives with us part-time. Then my mom gets pregnant, and I have a little brother. Then, just when I'm getting used to that, she gets pregnant again, and I have another little brother. I'm even getting used to that, and then my dad marries someone who is just a little older than my sister. And now she's having a baby, and I'm going to have another little brother. What do you mean I don't have stress in my life?"

Donna and I were a bit dumbfounded from Barry's speech. But she recovered quickly.

"You're right, Barry," she said calmly. "You really do have stress in your life. Try to do better on your report card next time."

BUILDING TRUST ONE DAY AT A TIME

Children have many fears and fantasies, but among them are that the new person, your new spouse, will steal you—their biological parent—away. They worry about the new person disrupting their relationship with you, fearing that he or she may push them out, leaving them abandoned again, as they felt they were before due to the divorce. They already lost their original family, and one of their parents may no longer be available to them on an ongoing basis, even with the advent of cell phones. They fear another abandonment, this time by you, and also from the new stepparent who has no biological tie to them. This is why you need to be present, and continually remind them of how important they are to you. In the best of circumstances, when the stepparent intervenes, even with constructive criticism, your child will feel attacked. If you are not there as a buffer, as someone to turn to, or as a source of protection, the child will only feel worse, and wonder why you are letting an essential interloper jump in and do what you should be doing.

This is a major step toward building trust for your child—trust in your new relationship, trust that it will last, and trust that the new family will embrace everyone.

This means both spouses taking all the time necessary to build relationships with each child. Spending positive time alone with each child shows that you care. Run your errands together and stop on the way for a treat, or go somewhere the child wants to go. Doing this shows the kid that you are trying to build a positive relationship. Spending individual time with your child can head off a lot of the needy, attention-seeking behavior and the animosity that occurs between your children, your new spouse, and your stepchildren. Your child needs to know that your other relationships are also important, but your willingness to take time to do something together points out their unique connection with you.

Your new spouse must also recognize that it is in the best interest of everyone for you to have this alone, bonding time. If your new spouse does not understand, cannot tolerate, or is threatened by you doing things occasionally with one or the other of the children, it will make everyone's life unpleasant. If they continually check to see when you are finished doing whatever you and the child are doing, everyone will become resentful, starting with you. The child may act out, the problems will escalate, and the family will not grow closer.

This is as true for teenagers as it is for older children who may want some individual parent time when they come visit, whether it is just to go shopping or spend some time having coffee and talking about their lives. Children just want an affirmation of how important they are to you.

My son Frank once made things quite clear for me.

"Dad, when I come to visit, I really like being with the other kids, and doing things all together as a family. I really like Donna and her kids. But I also like to do things with you once in a while, or just go off and talk. I really miss some of those times when it was just the two of us and we would go off together on trips. Spending a few hours alone with just you isn't quite the same, but it is sort of like those times. It's part of what I like about getting together, and as much as I like all of them, I resent it a little if we don't get to do that."

This focus on treating one child at a time as special seems to work better than trying to package any combination of them together, be it yours, your spouse's, or ours as a group. As your family grows, you have to adjust, but the individual relationships you cultivate will come together to form a layered, complex and satisfying family.

MORE BOUNDARIES, LESS CONFLICT

When it comes to blended families and managing relationships, the roles that each individual plays, the importance of staying within those roles, and the consequences when one oversteps them, are crucial to the success of that family.

We all need boundaries. Children develop them as infants, as they begin to learn who they are, where they are, what they need, and who can get those needs met. External boundaries help protect everyone, but particularly children as they are growing up, because they help them understand what they can and cannot do, as well as keeping them physically and emotionally safe. As children get older, boundaries slowly expand, protecting them and teaching them what is dangerous. It is important that children learn what is safe and what is not, whether it is physical places or people. In turn, children feel better knowing that their parents are in charge, will protect them and give them guidance about what they should or should not do.

Internal boundaries also help children differentiate themselves from others and teach them to respect other people as individuals rather than merely extensions of themselves. Knowing that a supportive adult is available helps children thrive, but if they realize they are not protected, it can cause long-term damage. When a child cannot trust a parent or a stepparent, or when he or she cannot depend on that adult for protection, it has very dire effects for everyone.

Boundaries can be violated in many ways. Allowing a child to run the show all the time, regardless of right or wrong, is a recipe for disaster. A parent ignoring a child's bad behavior is also a boundary violation, as is allowing a stepparent to discipline your child instead of doing it yourself, especially early in the relationship, or if the pair of them do not have a good relationship with each other. The most egregious boundary violations are the ones that go on to major physical or sexual abuse, which usually includes the biological parent's covert if not overt complicity in the process.

TAKING SIDES WHILE SUPPORTING EVERYONE

Because children usually do not want you to start a new family in the first place, they may show their anxiety by testing your commitment to them or by trying to sabotage your new relationship. They may provoke your new spouse to test you and see whether you will take their side or abandon them to support your new spouse. Life at this point may become even more chaotic when the new spouse's children are added to the mix, and each set of children will stir things up to see which side their own parent will take. Stop here. While all the children really want your attention, you need to focus first on your own children. You can certainly respond to their acting out with attention, but while you give it to them, you can point out what is going on, namely that they are acting out, and that they don't continually need to do that for you to still love them.

Not long after the wedding, Donna realized that Barry needed special time with her. He had always been the littlest kid growing up, and got teased because of his red hair. He was her baby. He was too young to take in what was happening and he felt vulnerable as a result of the divorce. Donna felt that she needed to stand up for him, even if his behavior was occasionally pushing the limits. But while Donna helped her son, she never made anyone feel wrong. She took Barry's side while still supporting the rest of the family.

It is not okay for a new person to come in and immediately make new rules that change everything that your family is used to. The ideas may be insightful and potentially helpful, but if you let your new spouse tell your child right away what to do you are giving up your parental role and responsibility. You are also taking sides while telling the child that what happened before was bad, including his or her past behavior.

The other message is that your child is not as important to you as the new person. Allowing your new partner to immediately run the show implies that you have chosen him or her over your child. It is your responsibility, and yours alone, to explain to these two people how important each of them is to you. You are the only one who can do that. No one else will do it for you!

If your new spouse doesn't understand what your child wants, what his or her behavior means, or why he or she wants you to do something, you need to explain it. If your new spouse finds some of your child's behavior upsetting and wants to jump in and change it, you may not be able to avoid a conflict, even if there is a good reason the child is behaving that way. One reason may well be that it just wasn't that important to you before, or that you tolerated it for a long time until someone started to point out that it was an issue. But again, you are the buffer and should not just let the new person intervene without being involved and explaining what you are doing and why you are doing it to both of them.

Donna always used to drive the kids to Sunday school, even before her divorce. One day after we were married, she was tired, and I offered to do it. Despite Donna encouraging him to go, Barry refused. I insisted, and the moment blew up. Later, Barry told Donna that he felt like it was supposed to be their private time together, and he didn't want to lose that or have someone else do it. While things may have been done a specific way in your spouse's family, you need to explain why things should be different now that you two are together.

If not, things between your child and your new spouse may quickly become problematic.

As you develop new rules and protocols together as a family, these episodes become less frequent. Your children are all you really have. Your new spouse is important, of course, but if you don't love, care for and protect your own children, no one else will. That's what being a parent is all about.

CHAPTER 12

WE'RE HAVING A BABY!

It's easy, especially in a second marriage with child and household obligations, career responsibilities and community and school connections, to get so caught up in 24/7 living that you take your new marriage—and spouse—for granted. Ideally, you will be with that person for a long, long time, even after the children grow up and leave home. With that in mind you have to make an effort to ensure that your present life is genuinely enjoyable and rewarding enough to get to the "rest of our lives." It is a little bit like putting money in the bank every day so that it will grow and be there for your retirement. That means taking time out of your normal activities to cultivate that relationship. No matter how demanding everything else may be, including the children, your job, your spouse's job, and the usual incidentals, you have to make time for your spouse and your relationship. In fact, you should be motivated to do a better job with this spouse and marriage than you did with the last one.

Just as you have to make special time to spend with your own children, you must block out time to spend with your new spouse. Even if your spouse is mature enough to take a step back to let you spend time with your children, you should not expect this of your new significant other all the time. If your spouse does not express any discontent and merely complies with everything you do, this probably isn't someone you want to be with in the long run anyway. Or, in another case, your spouse may be bottling up all associated emotions and blow up one day. When this happens you will hear all about how selfish, and inconsiderate you are, about how much he or she has done for you in the past couple of months or years without anything in return.

Work to maintain your new marriage on an ongoing and consistent basis. Long after the children have left and do not require constant maintenance, the person you married the second time around will hopefully still be there. It would be nice if you both liked being with each other.

A higher percentage of second marriages end in divorce than first marriages. Among the reasons for this is that many of the spouses feel neglected or shut out when their new spouse is spending too much time with his or her own children and not tending enough to the marriage. Work hard so that does not happen to you. Who knows? If you play your cards right and the stars are aligned in your favor, you and your spouse might choose to create a new family member.

THE DECISION

Many couples decide to expand their relationship by having a child, in effect adding "ours" to "his" and "hers." It may mean a first child for one of the new spouses, which is always of huge significance. It may be a question of sharing that experience with a loved one, in addition to sharing that spouse's other kids. It may even be a way to try and cement a relationship that seems fragile and tenuous. That is usually not very effective, and one of the partner's previous marriages may be more than enough evidence to demonstrate that point.

However, the long-term rewards of adding more children in a blended family are well worth considering. Combining three different batches of children, while difficult, to say the least, can be rewarding in ways unimaginable before they happen. As with everything else in life, problems will occur, whether you expect them or not, but all in all, gauging from my own experience and a multitude of patient evidence, the good vastly outweighs any real notion of bad.

But do not make that decision lightly. Adding another child is a serious, lifelong commitment. Are you about to become freed up from having your other children needing and demanding what seems like all your time and energy on a constant basis? Will a new baby mean curtailing your personal freedom? What about your combined financial resources? I can't answer these questions for you, but I encourage you to ask all the questions you can in order to be sure you are doing the right thing.

Once you do—jump! There is no perfect time to set out on this new adventure. If you wait until everything is in place, settled, and ready you will either be too old or no longer courageous enough to undertake the effort. Whatever happens, you will be older parents the second time around, the biological clock is usually ticking faster, which means there is pressure to do it sooner rather than later. There may also be anxiety and awareness about your own mortality. The concept of a ticking biological clock can be as worrying for men as it is for women. Nursery schools, and parks are full of middle-aged fathers who joke to each other about using their Medicare cards to get senior discount tickets at their kids' Little League games or ballet recitals. But those fathers are also one of the happier clubs in town.

If you thought getting married again was your biggest decision in life, wait until you are facing the prospect of having a new child with a new spouse!

PREPARING A NEW SET OF SIBLINGS

While you worry about those issues, your children, who may have just started to get comfortable about where they fit in with the new family, will be anxious about what their place will be in a new hierarchy that will include an additional child. They may have felt that they had some clout and tenure with you, their biological parent, but what will happen when you have two sets of children? Will you be pulled in two different directions, leaving your original children to observe the novelty of the new baby? And, what about the stepparent, who may have been nice to them before? Without a lifelong attachment, why would that person even care about them when another child comes into the picture? The scenario of a new child entering the family can be exciting, but it can also reignite ingrained fears of abandonment initially triggered by your divorce.

Once you and your spouse have decided to add a new child, you have to bring up the subject to your current children. Depending on their ages, their reactions will vary from being ecstatic about having a new toy to play with to being resentful that they will get an even smaller piece of their biological parent than they had before. Not to mention that they may have to give up their room and share with a sibling.

Almost no one automatically welcomes change of any sort, and this will be seen as a major change. Just because they are not ecstatic about the idea of a new addition when they first hear about it, it does not mean you should not go through with your plan. It does mean, though, that after a short time you should bring it up again, tell them that you really appreciate their input, and will want their help but basically have decided to do it anyway. After all, it is your life, and you and your new spouse will be together with the new additions long after the first batch of children leave home, although you should try to make the idea more tolerable for them from the start.

When Donna and I married, I went into it already knowing I wanted to have more children. Following my divorce, I had spent ten years commuting monthly between Texas and California in order to be with my son. I made sure that I saw at least one game per season in soccer and football, that I didn't miss his spelling bee finals, plays or every other significant date on his calendar. Each time I traveled west, from the time he was eight until he graduated high school at eighteen, I spent a couple of days in yet another hotel room, knowing no one else in the city except my son. In between visits, I planned what to do on the next one, always feeling as if I was trying to package a month's worth of parenting into two sacred days. In retrospect, we did plenty of fun things, but for ten years I always had the nagging feeling that I was really missing out on what parenting was all about, simply because I wasn't consistently there. I was left romanticizing about what living with and raising my own child full-time would really be like.

My desire to have more children influenced who I dated, which meant excluding people that I am sure were wonderful, and with whom I might have gotten involved had we not had a fundamental disagreement about our future. Throughout this entire time, I never wavered in my desire to have another child. Donna was happy with the two kids she had, but the idea eventually grew on her.

Looking back, we can both agree that having more kids on top of the ones we already had was more work than we bargained for and we were exhausted a great deal of the time. Donna felt like no one was happy with what she was doing, despite the fact that she was taking care of everybody. The more she tried to do, the more everyone complained and seemed to feel neglected. When Donna went to see a psychiatrist (not me!) he joked with her, but his words were telling.

"The problem is that your breasts aren't big enough. You just don't have enough milk for everyone." Metaphorically speaking, he might have been right, despite the fact that at the time three of our children were teenagers.

But all along, Donna and I never felt that we were not living in a loving environment or doubted that we would find a way through. And now, I wouldn't have given up any of it or any one of them. Love goes a long, long way when it's genuine.

BONDING VS. BABYSITTING

The first reaction that all children have when they learn that their family is going to add a new child is to get very excited. The next reaction, even when they are living with both biological parents is usually anxiety, fear, and jealousy, driven by the questions, which are also asked by children in non-divorced families:

"What will happen to me?"

"What did I do wrong so that they want to add someone else?"

"I wasn't good enough so they have to add someone else."

"If I was good enough or if they were happy enough with me, they wouldn't want to add another child."

These reactions typify children who are aware that all the attention that used to be focused on them and that they now share in a blended family will soon be directed to someone they did not invite, and most probably did not want. While this feeling of being displaced and abandoned is an issue for all children, in a blended family the children are already sensitized to the focus on them being interrupted, and the feeling that they are not as important to their biological parents as they once had been. This means that the traditional "what's wrong with me" questions which arise with a new baby are made even worse by the child's post-divorce experience of actual abandonment.

There is no simple solution to their fear, anxiety, and concerns. The best thing you can do is to constantly reassure them that they are important, that you love them, that they are part of the new family, and that you need their help to make it all work. Your children and stepchildren also need to know that your decision to have another child is not about them, but rather that you want to share the love you have for them with a new child. Over time, if you repeat it enough, the message should sink in.

The effect of a new child will be obvious on the children who are living in the home, but it also has an effect on the children who just come to visit at prearranged times and are not permanent residents. All of them should be privy to what is going on, how things are progressing, and how you think life will be for everyone after the baby arrives. They should be reassured again and again that a new child is not a negative reflection on them, or an indication that they will be replaced. At least one of their own parents is also the biological parent of the new child, and they may have concerns about their parent's health as well as the health of the baby.

This is particularly true in regards to the health of the mother, whether she is their own biological mother or not. Having been surprised by the divorce and the way it affected them, the children will also be concerned about how another child might destabilize their lives.

Helping to prepare your children and stepchildren for a new sibling is not unlike what you did when you were preparing them for the new marriage. Allow them to pick out things for the new baby's room and let them share your excitement as the process moves forward. Make sure they get to see the sonograms and let them feel the baby's kicks. Let everyone be involved in picking a name. Make it a team effort.

When Donna first found out the sex of the baby, she was very excited, and told all the kids. At first, I asked not to be told because I didn't know the sex of my first child and I didn't want to know about this one, either. Her kids were so excited that they told their own dad, so everyone knew but me. At that point, I realized that if her ex-husband knew the sex of my new child, I should too, so I gave in and they told me.

Your first children need to feel part of this new family, and that they are related to and connected to their new sibling. This is really best done if the children are involved with the baby as soon as possible. Take them to the hospital when the baby comes. Let them play with the new baby or help you bottle feed the new child. Eventually your older children will bond with their new brother or sister. When you go home, you can further this process by having them help you with activities that involve the baby, whether it is preparing food, feeding, playing, or even pushing the stroller.

When our first baby was born, the other children got really excited and enjoyed playing with him and watching him do things. They both quickly felt like they were partially responsible for him turning out okay.

But partially is as far as it should go. You and your spouse wanted a new child, not your children. They just happen to be living with you, are dependent on you and are trying to survive as best they can, given everything that has already happened in their life. Why should they have to take care of your new children because you decided to further complicate their life? Do not make them take care of your new children so that you can do other things, even if those things seem important to you or to the family in general. Ask them if they would like to help out, but give them the choice. Offer to pay them to babysit or to help out if you need them to. This way, they are treated in the same manner as a paid nanny or babysitter from the outside, which you would have to look into hiring anyway if they were not around. That gives the older children a choice, rather than pushing them into doing something they may not want to do, or making them feel obligated to do something that interferes with their own schedule. By giving them the choice of being involved, for pay or not, you reinforce for them that they are individuals with their own priorities and life and that they are as important to you as the new baby is. They may want to do it anyway and volunteer but that is different than making it a requirement. If they feel compelled to babysit or care for their new sibling, they may grow resentful of the baby and feel that this child is in the family at their expense.

One evening at the last minute, Donna and I wanted to go to a party. It was too late to call one of our usual babysitters. Instead we asked, i.e. told, our older kids to babysit. They became angry, then resentful.

"We already have plans, why do we have to change them to babysit?"

After pushing them some more to help out, we realized they were right. The new babies were our children, not theirs. They had plans, which were just as important to them as ours were to us. Donna and I realized that if we couldn't plan ahead, regardless of whether we offered to pay them or not, we, not our kids, should have to deal with the consequences.

We stayed home that night, like many, many others. Years later, I don't remember what the party was even about or who was hosting it, but I'm sure I can remember spending a wonderful evening at home with the family I loved.

PART 4

LESSONS LEARNED

1. Being a stepparent is always difficult but it can also bring great rewards.

2. You are marrying a family, not just a person.

3. If you don't like the person's kids, change yourself, or it will never work for anyone.

4. Include the children in your activities.

5. Try to get along with if not befriend the ex-spouse. Everyone will benefit.

6. It is important to recognize that when the stepchild gets mad and focuses it on you, it may not be about you, but the role you play and that you are there.

7. The biological parent is responsible for raising his or her own children.

8. When children are struggling with transitions, they need their parents even more.

9. The long-term rewards of adding more children in a blended family are well worth considering.

10. Prepare your children and stepchildren for a new sibling.

YOURS, MINE, AND OURS: TROUBLESHOOTING FOR THE FUTURE

CHAPTER 13

FROM CHURCH TO CHECKBOOK

On the first Thanksgiving morning Donna and I spent together as one family, I grabbed a football and told Frank to get ready to leave for our annual game of touch football, which we played every year with several other parents and their kids. It was a fun tradition. One of the kids was Frank's best friend, and most of the others were his age. This year, just as we were about to leave, Barry, who at ten years old was four years younger than Frank, said he wanted to join us. My knee jerk response was to say no. It was our tradition; he was too little, and I thought that having him there would detract from everyone else's good time. Eventually, between his persistence, his mother's urging and Frank's saying "It's not that big a deal," we all went. To my surprise and delight, it worked out well. No one else really cared and everyone had a great time. Barry, who was little but very fast and aggressive, scored the first touchdown. He felt great, his mother was much happier with me for including him and Frank was able to bask in having a successful little brother. Plus, it helped Barry and I move along a little in our relationship.

BLENDING HOLIDAYS, CULTURES, AND TRADITIONS

Traditions, special events and cultural rituals are a major part of what helps to organize people's lives, and in turn creates structure, meaning, and connectedness between individuals, their subgroup, and society. Our individual and collective traditions distinguish us from one another. These cultural, political and religious rituals, rites of passage, and celebrations of events all serve to define us, especially as family units. They act as mileposts in our lives while letting others understand our expectations and values.

As Tevye in *Fiddler on the Roof* pointed out, every family invariably has its own traditions and unique idiosyncratic sets of behavior, informing others about who its members are. Traditions, rituals, and the celebration of special events are particularly important for children because they help develop their identity, create an understanding of who they are and where they come from, what their boundaries are, and where they are going. It is important to include parents and grandparents in these special occasions because their participation provides a longitudinal picture of the family's heritage.

Today, in spite of our transient society, most people still get together for major events, such as births, graduations, popular holidays and funerals. They even travel long distances to do so. But as families blend, they develop their own rituals around major and minor occasions, all of which children may get excited about.

Following a divorce, a splintered family may try to salvage some of their former rituals to retain the structure and feeling of closeness they once had, but the celebrations are not like they used to be. Part of the original family is often missing, the ex being the other parent, and a major dilemma is often whether to include that parent and the extended family, such as the ex's parents, who are the grandparents of the shared children. When the biological parents continue celebrating these occasions it helps everyone remember that there was a family that had traditions before the divorce. This reinforces for the children that what happened was not their fault. It also helps to acknowledge and validate good feelings that the children may have had about those events in the past, although it can also trigger off sad memories of what once was.

When a blended family with two new and different parents, two sets of children, and two sets of traditions blend together the major differences which exist may not be apparent until after an explosion occurs. It is only when a clash of cultures exposes these differences that they can be looked at, talked about, and new ones developed.

Every year since we have been together, we get a Baskin-Robbins ice cream cake to celebrate birthdays. We have been doing it for so long that if it did not happen everyone would be surprised, upset and disappointed. There is no magic in it; it is just a nice tradition—our tradition and something to treasure and hold onto.

If only it were always so easy.

On the first Christmas Donna and I spent together, we had all the children. At six in the morning I was still sleeping, and was roused not by "Santa and eight tiny reindeer," but by screaming, shouting, and a racket. I slowly awoke to see what was wrong, and discovered that by the time we had gotten out of bed to hand out the presents, see the kids excited reactions and take pictures of them with the items we had spent so much time thinking about, planning, putting together, and wrapping, they had already gone downstairs and opened everything. I was upset, angry, and aghast.

In my family, the children never opened anything until the parents came down. Then everyone ate breakfast together, got the cameras out, and slowly unwrapped the stockings and the presents, one by one. This was to allow the children and the parents to savor each present, and let the parents bask in the glow of what good parents they were to have gotten the kids what they wanted. After all, what was the purpose of buying all those presents if you couldn't share the kids' excitement and see their faces when they opened them? It also meant that everyone got to eat breakfast, and the entire morning was spent opening presents. That was very different from the notion that if the kids were busy opening them and having a great time, the parents could sleep later than they otherwise would.

Donna grew annoyed and upset with me. According to her, the kids were having a good time, really excited about their presents, and were happily playing with them. If we said anything it would ruin their fun. She didn't think it was such a big deal. We hadn't talked about it; in fact, we hadn't thought about it, and after all of my huffing and puffing, she just said, "Who is to say what is right or wrong?" Besides, she was tired and was glad they were having a good time together, and that meant we could sleep a little longer without worrying about them. I knew she was probably right, but my conditioning kept telling me I wasn't so sure. I had some work to do on the subject before the next Christmas arrived.

You need to recognize, accept, and begin to modify the old ways until they finally work for everyone. Unfortunately, in the heat of the moment, and if you have already established ideas or a history of how things should be, it is disconcerting to wake up—literally—and find that things are being done differently. There are obviously many different ways to celebrate but when something you are not aware of suddenly happens and leaves you caught in the middle without warning, the realization that it is not a big deal and can be worked out does not always seem to help. What is important is that when you do have one of those events, you both talk about it later, try to understand what happened, and move on.

A special event should be commemorated as everyone had been accustomed to until someone presents a very different way of doing it that you all discuss and decide to change. I can assure you that you will never anticipate every situation that will come up but someone will, so be ready when they do. Then, if it doesn't immediately agree with you, try not to blow up while it is happening just because it doesn't fit the historical expectations of you and your family. Instead agree that you both will try to understand what is going on and modify it accordingly.

In a second marriage with a blended family, new rules, discipline, rituals and traditions can also be worked out, but you do not have the luxury of many years to do it, nor the ease of beginning with a very young, more impressionable child as you did in your first marriage. On top of that, it requires even more understanding, tolerance, and the inclusion of everyone as the process unfolds. Inclusion does not mean that parents need to do what the children say they want, but it does mean that the children's input should be heard, and acknowledged. It also means that the reasons for certain actions are clear to the children, even if it is not what they suggested or wanted.

There is never a time, no matter how badly a child may behave, that warrants saying to anybody—the children, or your new spouse—that things were bad before the new marriage and now that I am the new parent here, we are going to live by my rules, which will make them better. That type of behavior belongs in a bad movie, not in real life. But I mention it because I have seen it happen all too often. When for some reason a parent gets it in his or her head that positive changes and new rules will begin "as soon as the ring goes on my finger," or the other spouse says that "we will now live by my rules," we are talking about a recipe for disaster. You should never use the threat of saying to the child that you are going to have to go and live with your dad or mom if you don't do what I say, or live by my rules. That is very upsetting to the child and will undoubtedly be to your new spouse, and is often, if not always, counterproductive. The underlying message is that the child is not wanted by anyone, or is only loved conditionally, which further adds to the fear of being abandoned again. Children should be allowed to flow between their biological parents, with some effort made to establish similar rules and similar consequences when they are with either parent.

Every blended family will face its challenges as it tries to combine different traditions and cultures under the same roof. In the case of religious holidays, they were never a big deal for Donna or me, but I always had a Christmas tree growing up. Donna never did, and thought it was a little much. After we got together, we did it for a few years. Then the little kids decided we shouldn't do it but now that they are away at school and come home every so often, they want to do it each year for the holidays. They think it makes the house feel cozier. Go figure!

PAST, PRESENT, AND FUTURE

When it comes to activities you may have enjoyed over the years before you remarried—golf, stamp collecting, hunting, bowling, bird watching, music, or anything else—there is no reason for you to give them up, certainly not entirely. These pursuits have brought you hours of pleasure and satisfaction, and have come to identify who you are to those who know you best. This means that just because you are now married, even to someone with children, you should not give them all up, even if your new spouse is not always interested in them. Getting married involves blending your life with another person and his or her family. That means sacrifice and compromise, but giving up who you are is not part of the deal. In fact, one of the things that made you attractive in the first place might have been your many interests and passions. So why not try to include your new family members in your activities?

Whenever appropriate, involve your new spouse and stepchildren in your preferred activities. That's a big part of developing a new, truly blended family where everyone feels they are a part of what each other likes to do, even if it's just the routine activities that are part of your normal day. Sharing doesn't have to be exotic. It may just be just running errands with a stepchild and stopping in the middle to do something different—something special—besides the usual routine. Children need to feel you recognize something special about them. Perhaps one or more of your stepchildren will eventually come to share your hobbies and interests and enjoy participating in them with you. That can become a lifelong source of enjoyment, bonding, and personal growth for both of you.

When I was single, I got involved in duck hunting with some friends. It was fun and I became serious enough about it to even have my own dog. When Donna and I came together, I took Barry with me once and we had a great time. We even shot a few ducks that he proudly brought home for his mom to cook. To this day, when he comes home during the hunting season he always calls me ahead of time to set up a hunting trip and we have a great time hunting together.

GOING DUTCH IN THE TWENTY-FIRST CENTURY

Numerous studies demonstrate and family therapists will largely agree that couples in both first and second marriages fight over money more than any other single issue, including children and in-laws. In blended families, where newlyweds often face the financial fallout from two divorces, the issue may be even more intense.

Working out finances is an ongoing challenge and a frequent source of conflict—real and imagined—for most couples. This is particularly true for parents in new blended families, who face the dilemma of who should pay for what, for whom, and for whose children—and how much?

The financial responsibilities of my new family seemed overwhelming to me at first. I thought I was doing okay, managing my one part-time child and child-support payments, while maintaining my own lifestyle, which up until that point had been relatively simple. But then all of a sudden I had a new wife and two more kids. Every time we would go out to eat, even for a pizza, I was tallying up the cost and not enjoying myself. I had grown up with Depression era parents who always had me look at the price side of the menu, so it made me anxious that the three kids would never split anything. They would get upset because I was always looking at who got what. My nerves about money made them feel like I was treating them differently than how they had grown up.

At the time, my stepson, Barry, thought that I didn't really want him to have any extra shrimp without sharing it with everyone else, which just reminded him again that I wasn't his dad. Now that he has his own child, I think he can realize how complex it can be to get involved with someone who has two kids and have to think about paying for some of their stuff.

Couples without children often have difficulty determining who will pay for what, beginning with household expenses, vacations, and even community property items. When children are added to the mix, the sensitive question of paying for children's expenses surfaces almost immediately. What's yours and what's mine becomes an issue regardless of how much money either spouse actually has or makes. In fact, due to the financial repercussions of having gone through one divorce and possibly fearing another, most people with any significant assets will not want to merge their finances right away, in lieu of finding other ways to share everyday costs. That is just as well, as there is no automatic or obvious way to manage or merge your finances with those of your new spouse. There are several basic concepts to consider, including children, assets, income, and monthly child support, if either spouse is receiving or paying.

In general, it seems best if each spouse remains responsible for his or her own children's expenses, such as clothing, tuition, medical bills, and other basics, some of which may have been paid for by the ex, and probably will and should be after the new marriage. The new spouse may want to help out, but that should be their choice and not an expectation or a requirement, which will only risk future misunderstanding and resentment. Since there is no formula for this, open communication is the best approach. So how many checkbooks will you need?

How household and living expenses are divided, apart from the children, will differ from couple to couple. Situations vary from one extreme where a spouse traditionally pays for everything to where everything is split down the middle and you and your spouse go Dutch. Between these two extremes are situations where each spouse puts an amount into a monthly household account. It could be an equal amount or a percentage of personal income, or even go into a family account. When you go on a family vacation, each parent can pay for his or her own child or one may choose to pay for the whole trip from a separate account. When the structure is set up ahead of time it helps limit the conflict that will occur when crises arise and it can be modified over time or as circumstances change.

When the biological parent pays for his or her own children, the stepparent does not feel used or pushed into doing things, and can choose what to do rather than feel compelled to provide immediately for the stepchildren. That helps to minimize conflicts about whose kids get what, as long as they are treated equally when they are all together at home or on trips. For a significant time, whenever possible, the biological parent should assume the same financial responsibility for his or her own children from the first marriage, and should continue to do so until the new spouse chooses to willingly accept more financial responsibility. Despite the fact that you married a package, that package was supposedly self-sustaining. In truth, the stepchildren and the biological parent were apparently surviving before you entered the picture, and your involvement was primarily with your new spouse and your feelings for each other. If one or the other feels trapped in having to pay for the other person's children, it sets the stage for both parties to become unhappy in the long run.

If there is significant income disparity between the two spouses and one is getting married in order to be taken care of, the marriage, itself, may be at risk. Expectations must be laid out clearly beforehand. This includes questions of who should pay for college and what type. I have seen patients who are still mad because the stepparent's child got to go to prestigious, expensive colleges while they had to attend a cheaper state school, although they did better academically.

We have heard many cautionary tales, like from the wife who never looked at her marital financial situation until she had been married for fifteen years and found out that her second husband was spending a lot of money at the casinos while she paid for all of their living expenses, including for his kids and ex-wife.

I've met many men who resent their second wives expecting them to pay for everything. Unfortunately, it's rare when I meet a couple that has accepted the financial challenges of their new blended family, communicated openly and honestly and made the best of their shared situation. It's up to you. If you really love someone, you'll make the right choices.

Parental anxiety surfaces all the time and in strange ways. As our two babies were coming, Donna asked me one day, out of the blue, if I had life insurance. I had only a small policy from when I was a part-time parent, and she flipped out.

"If something happened to you, I'd grieve and be sad, but there is no reason that I should be poor, too."

That triggered off a call to a life insurance salesman. While I couldn't guarantee much in life, at least I could arrange to leave my family taken care of, just in case I died trying my best to love them.

CHAPTER 14

BIGGER AND BETTER

Learning to share things with other people can be very difficult (remember kindergarten?), but if you live with other people, it's something everyone needs to learn. This is especially true in blended families. Sharing does not mean that the older kid always has to give up something for the younger child any more than it means that the older one can always take things from that same younger sibling. It does not mean that the child who visits occasionally should get everyone else's stuff to use because he or she is only there part-time. Genuine sharing means that everyone has value. It means being willing to help out or give in a little. Sharing toys or favorite objects is not much different than sharing your pet, and ultimately sharing your parent. As you blend two families together, everyone—children and adults alike—needs to learn to share.

After Donna and I had been living together for six months, Frank came to stay with us for the summer. Barry was playing in his room with two friends when he and Frank got into an argument, so Frank left. The dog, which I had gotten Frank six years before, and who stayed with me, was also in the room. Frank called him, but Barry told the dog to stay in the room. This went on for a few minutes and the poor dog was bouncing back and forth, not knowing what to do. I felt terrible, and didn't know any more than the dog. Finally, the dog stayed with Barry. I felt terrible for Frank. After a few tense moments, the dog wandered off and ended up playing with Frank. Soon enough, all the boys ended up playing together again. I know that if I had put myself in the middle of it, things would have escalated, and they all would have remained upset about it for quite some time. Sometimes the true spirit of sharing reveals itself without any help from us adults.

LETTING GO: RECOGNIZING LIMITS WITH YOUR CHILDREN

Powerless is a term often used when discussing addiction, but it can also describe how you feel as a parent when your biological children are living with your ex or even when they live with you, but spend significant time with the other parent. You quickly realize that divorce means reduced input and that you may not have direct control over what happens to the children you share. Like it or not, this is the reality for many people after a divorce. Unless you have a reasonable relationship and good communication with the other parent, you need to recognize and understand that the only parental influence you can exercise occurs when the children are with you.

This may seem unfair if not unpalatable, but as a divorced parent, you need to appreciate that as much as you might wish, you cannot cram a whole year's worth of parenting into a summer month or a holiday visit. How your ex behaves with your children is not your responsibility. You cannot control it, and you cannot be responsible for how it affects your kids. You can only hope for the best and be yourself.

Children will learn the most from you by spending time with you, watching you, learning what is important to you, and role modeling. They will learn about the things you value if you simply act on those things rather than talking about them while you do something else, or disparage the other parent. Children quickly see through the "do as I say, but not as I do" approach, and also recognize how you live and what is important to you. You do not need to frantically cram everything that you want your child to know into a few days or weeks just because your time with them is limited. In fact, you must accept the situation, relax and enjoy your children when they are with you. The truth is, even if you were still married and living with their other parent, they would pick and choose aspects of both your behaviors that they wanted, and probably ignore other pieces of your behavior that they did not like or did not fit for them. Plus, just because both their parents lived together under the same roof, it wouldn't mean that your children would want to interact with each of you in some democratic, equal fashion.

Your impact with your stepchildren is also very limited in the short term. You are not their real parent, which they will point out again and again, and your only power with them emanates from the support your new spouse displays in implementing decisions that involve them. This lack of power, which often feels like you have little or no say, is a very difficult issue for many newly minted stepparents, and a truth they often find hard to accept. As a stepparent, you may try to discipline your stepchildren, but as we discussed earlier, that is really much better accomplished by going through their biological parent. You can suggest to the stepchildren what to do, but if those statements come out as orders, they are frequently met with resistance from them and an unpleasant feeling of powerlessness for you. Recognize this early on and you will save yourself—and everyone else—a lot of frustration and heartache. Even years later, you may find that whenever you try to jump into a situation you become the odd person out and your new spouse and children gang up against you. Like most issues that arise in blending families, it will improve over time, but you cannot force things to adhere to your agenda, no matter how frustrated, disappointed or angry you may feel at the moment. There is little you can do, except talk to your new spouse about your thoughts and feelings and explain why you would like them to support you in at least getting your opinions and ideas heard.

At times in his adolescence, Barry and I would go at it and he would talk or yell at me in ways that I did not like. I thought he was also setting a bad example for our younger kids. I would scold him about it, which only escalated the tension. Whenever I talked to Donna and she took his side, I became further infuriated. I realized that it was better just to talk about it to her when Barry wasn't around. That gave her a chance to deal with him casually, which became a much more effective method.

Let go! Reconsider your own agenda and live your life. No one is keeping score, unless it's you.

DEALING WITH YOUR EX-SPOUSE

No matter how long a blended couple is together, there are potential crisis points in their relationship, and one of those is one—or both—of your exes' remarriage. Just as everyone seems to be adapting nicely to your new blended family, your ex-spouse decides to remarry. This may become a crisis and upset your children all over again because it is another reminder that their original family has ended, and that now both their biological parents may not be as

interested in them as they had been before. More important, the new marriage may change your relationship with
your children.

The remarriage of your ex means that there is now another
person involved with your children when they visit their other
parent. That person may be injecting a new point of view and
trying to install a new agenda in that home, which can make
the ex harder rather than easier to deal with. The ex may have
married someone who thinks that you have done a poor job
of parenting and sees your children as a new project or as people who need to be saved. For others, the ex may have married
someone who wants more input or control with your children, which suddenly stirs up what had been a relatively stable situation. The children are once again unpleasantly caught
in the middle between you and the ex's new spouse, who is
telling them how to behave. If this is the case, the children
will sadly end up as the losers.

The resolution is always to try and communicate with the
other parent although that is often easier said than done. In
truth, if the two of you could communicate well about issues
such as the ones you now disagree about, you would probably still be together rather than divorced. Still, the better the
communication before issues arise, and the more time, notice,
and reasons you give for why you do things, the better it usually is for everyone. It also helps to try befriending your ex's
new spouse, or if that cannot be done, to be civil to him or
her. Remember that nothing is usually improved by your new
spouse arguing with your ex, or your ex's new spouse arguing
with you.

At times like this, it is more helpful to have your new
spouse be supportive of you, your efforts, and the pressure
you're put under when this remarriage occurs.

A patient once told me, "My ex-husband and I were really getting along well until he got remarried. His wife couldn't have kids, and basically wanted my kids. Within a short time he was questioning everything I did, double checking stuff, getting tight on the money, looking for issues, and trying to go back to court to change the custody arrangement. I really saw it as being pushed by her rather than him, but there was nothing I could do. The kids were really upset and confused. All of a sudden they go from a dad who doesn't come very often to one who is buying them all kinds of stuff all the time, and taking them to Astroworld every chance he gets. It really got the fighting started all over again."

The simple solution would be for you and your new spouse to act as friends, and do what you can to support each other in raising the children you have in common. This is ideal and what the courts mean when they refer to "the best interests of the child." While encouraging one biological parent not to speak badly about the other, or even tell kids the specifics of the divorce, is the right thing to do, it does not happen often enough. People simply talk too much and don't consider the effect it will have on their children.

In my case, Donna's ex was comfortable with me and did not think that I was undermining his authority or his own parenting. This meant that if there were issues, and Donna wasn't around, he would sometimes tell me what he wanted because he trusted that I would tell Donna. I didn't always agree with what he did, but most of the time I had the good sense to stay out of it.

As the most recent addition to your new spouse's family, it is best to try and get along with the ex. Try to understand this person a little, be civil, and if possible try to actually be friendly. If you already have children, you know what it is like to have your children being at least partially managed by someone else, particularly a surrogate you did not choose. It therefore should behoove you and help everyone out the most, if you can at least stay out of the middle of issues that come up between your new spouse and his or her ex. In all probability those were their issues long before you entered the picture, and will remain so well into the future, whether you are there or not. Once again, let go. Let them resolve their own stuff. The most helpful thing you can do is keep your distance and provide your new spouse with support, if and when he or she asks for it.

It is in everyone's interest—your new spouse, his or her children and even the ex—if you become friendly with the stepchildren's absent parent. For example, when problems develop with the ex's children, you can be relied upon as a resource rather than just another person to fight with. This is particularly so if there is a communication problem between the two of them, which is too often the case. In reality, the ex really did you a favor, and freed up your new spouse to be with you. Because your spouse's ex is now physically absent in your new blended family, you have the opportunity to be involved with your now spouse and his or her biological children, who you might otherwise not have known and who may make your life richer and better. Why should you not be appreciative and friendly toward that person?

Donna's ex-husband often came inside our house when he dropped off the kids after doing something with them. Often, it would be at dinnertime when we are all sitting down to eat or waiting for the kids to get started. He would often go to the pantry to see what there was to snack on (like another kid), and hang around and talk for a while. Sometimes, Donna or I asked him to join us for dinner or have a drink with us before he took off. Our openness made him comfortable and I think it left him feeling that he was not being maligned or negatively discussed when he wasn't there. His children got a sense that there was an easy transition between what went on with their biological parents and stepparents, and made it easier for them to go from house to house. The obvious transparency between all of us meant that both of their parents were attending to their needs. They were not in the middle, not being fought over, or required to relay information between parents. Unfortunately, it did not undo the fact that the children felt that it was still somewhat unnatural, and that no place felt completely theirs.

At the same time, it was very puzzling for Frank. My son could not imagine divorced parents who could interact freely without an ongoing level of animosity or without him being in the middle. All he had ever known were parents who never communicated and lived in different places, and when his father visited, his mother avoided any interaction with him, leaving him without a shred of family togetherness.

While the ex may initially see you as a threat, you can help minimize that by not pointing out how bad things were before you came along or how this person is continuing to handle things poorly right now. If you approach it in this way, there is no reason that the ex should not begin to see you as a helper in raising his or her children, which ultimately should be appreciated. Hopefully, the reassurance of no longer stressing about being a single parent will allow the ex and your new spouse to get along better. You can encourage your new spouse to hassle your stepchildren's other parent less, help out financially and try to be there for the children when their biological parent cannot be. Becoming sociable with your spouse's ex can be a win-win situation for your stepchildren. If you all get along, the children will be happier.

Unfortunately, some exes are very difficult to deal with. When that happens, the best thing you can do is let your new spouse do the communicating. Provide emotional support, but if at all possible, stay out of the actual conflict.

Despite claiming otherwise, children love both of their parents. When you and your spouse's ex get into a fight, your stepchildren may feel torn. In these situations, blood may be thicker than water and they could end up supporting the parent you are fighting rather than you.

A patient once described to me how he became the bad guy.

"It was really kind of shocking. She told me about all her problems with her ex: what he was like, what he had done to her, how difficult he was to deal with, and how he was with the children. When he would come and get the kids, I saw what she was talking about and agreed with her. I couldn't stand the guy. I started pushing to get her custody situation changed. All of a sudden, she gets mad at me and says my interfering is messing up the kids, and to stay out of it. It took me a while to realize that it was not my business, and that I shouldn't have been involved in the first place."

Never forget that while you love one of your stepchildren's biological parents, the children love them both. That other parent may have some bad traits, may be hurtful to the child at times, and the child may not always like that parent, but it is not your role to point those things out. You should not be critical in any way of your stepchildren's absent parent or point out any shortcomings, even though this person's actions may disappoint or hurt his or her own child. You can be supportive of the child and sensitive to hurt feelings, but that is very different than criticizing someone the child loves. That will only remind the child that his or her original family is gone. It may also push you to be viewed as a divisive wedge in the original family. Children often idealize their first family, no matter how bad the situation may have been. No one, including the child's biological parent, should talk ill of another parent. And it's never your battle to fight.

These are good reasons not to be critical of the absent parent, even when criticism is clearly deserved. As children get older they often start to realize what their biological parents are really like, see their faults, and understand why their own parents are no longer together. That is a process that occurs best without your critical input—unless you are asked to give it.

WELCOMING VISITING OR ABSENT CHILDREN INTO THE FAMILY

When you are the non-biological parent living with someone else's children and your own children come home for a visit, having everyone together at the same time can be awkward. It is another one of those situations where either everyone is happy or, whatever you do, everyone is unhappy and it's all your fault. During and after the visit, you need to avoid treating your biological children in a special manner that causes resentment among your stepchildren and may also upset your new spouse.

It is difficult for a divorced parent to describe the pain of being involved with someone else's children while your own children are not around. Those feelings never really leave, so when they visit it is hard not to treat them as special and different, particularly if it's been awhile. All of your children will do better when everyone is treated equally, but that does not mean they won't try to get special treatment, and you may occasionally provide it in spite of your better judgment.

While you may be inclined to give your own child special treatment, that is usually a guarantee that everyone else will be upset, including the child you are unfairly indulging.

When your children visit, try to have everyone be involved with them from the beginning. It may seem unfair, or appear to close out the opportunity to give the visiting child a sense of being special, but ultimately, for a family unit to develop with trust and respect, everyone needs to feel that they are just as important as everyone else. It is obviously important to spend time alone with each of your children, but it is also important that they spend time with the other kids and that you all are involved together. Let your blended family really become blended, in the best sense of the word.

One of the things I had always done with Frank when he visited me was to take him to the local go-kart track, where we had great races and loads of fun. The first few times Frank visited after Donna and I got together, I would suggest doing that with him, only to have Barry get upset. Naturally, he wanted to go, too. Eventually, I included him and to my surprise, it did not detract at all from our enjoyment. In fact it helped all three of us get closer.

As you build on the positivity of each visit, your children will want to come more often and get involved with everyone. The best approach is probably to try and spend a little special time with your children, and then involve them with everyone. The truth is that your children will probably be as happy about that as everyone else is. You are not as much fun to be with all the time as other kids, and the only one who feels strange about it in the beginning is you.

The first Christmas vacation we spent together, Donna, her two kids, my dog and I went to the airport to pick up Frank. We ended up staying at her house for two days. Then I tried to get Frank to go home with me—and the dog.

"You all don't have to," Donna said. "You can stay here." Her children agreed, and Frank said that he would also like to stay. That upset me, and I tried to reassert my point to Frank that we had a home, and that we should go be our own separate little family. Frank held his ground and ended up staying. I took the dog went back to my place. At four a.m., having made whatever point I thought I needed to make about Frank and I still being our own family unit, I called Donna and said I was coming back. She was okay with it. I was chagrined, and the kids didn't say much either way except that they thought I had been silly. It wasn't my first time and certainly not the last.

CHAPTER 15

LESSONS LEARNED

I've spent decades trying to understand, chronicle and explain my experience blending two families together. As you may know from your own story, diverse people from different backgrounds, with contrasting habits and traditions, come together because two of those people—the responsible adults, in fact—can't help loving each other, and despite the odds, they decide to marry, uniting their families under one roof—children, pets and all—and then hold their breath and hope for the best.

Crazy, I know. But many of us do it anyway, and in my case, I have never had a single regret. My experience is not unique. We know the numbers. Half of all marriages end in divorce and many of those people go on to remarry, sometimes two or three more times, often adding more children each time they do.

I know I've been lucky. Most of the credit goes to my wife and our children. But in all honesty, and with a dose of humility, I will pat myself on the back for putting in a lot of time, energy and effort to make it all work. I really tried! That doesn't mean I didn't make a ton of mistakes. You've already witnessed plenty of that. There are so many things I wish I hadn't done, or would have done differently.

As a psychiatrist, you'd think my special training would've taught me a thing or two and that I wouldn't have made so many mistakes. I guess all that education did help me realize when I had messed up and it helped me learn from my mistakes and move on. Contrary to what my children may have thought during certain years, I was just a human being, an ordinary guy just doing his best to figure it all out as he went along.

LESSONS LEARNED

1. Celebrate special events and occasions with everyone, and try to develop traditions for your new family.

2. Recognize, accept, and begin to modify the old ways until they finally work for everyone.

3. Children should be allowed to flow between their biological parents, with some effort made to establish similar rules and similar consequences when they are with either parent.

4. Whenever appropriate, involve your new spouse and stepchildren in your preferred activities.

5. Children need to feel you recognize something special about them.

6. It seems best if each spouse remains responsible for his or her own children's expenses.

7. Genuine sharing means that everyone has value.

8. Divorce means reduced input and that you may not have direct control over what happens to the children you share.

9. Reconsider your own agenda and live your life.

10. Never forget that while you love one of your stepchildren's biological parents, the children love them both.

A NOTE OF HOPE

I am still learning. As a matter of fact, every day one of our kids manages to point out what I did wrong or what I still need to work on. Sometimes they are right; sometimes they are not, but I always try to listen. Once in awhile, to my utter delight, one of the kids points out that I have become a better parent only because of his or her help. Occasionally, someone will even tell me I did something right. I think this means that we are all learning and can keep learning from each other.

That means you will no longer have total responsibility for everything and everyone. Your children may have two more positive, caring and supportive adults involved with them than just you and their other biological parent. They can also get positive input from the older and younger kids they feel connected to.

Divorce does not often bring out the best in people and the effect on children is long lasting. But you can repair some of that damage. A positive blended family is one way to help that process happen.

Sometimes when we least expect it, we discover that all the hard work we put into trying to make a tough situation work out has actually paid off and our children have fared better than we ever imagined. I hope this book will inspire you to make your blended family a happy and healthy one in spite of all the challenges. May you be as blessed as I have been.

I was going through my desk the other day and found this fifteen-year-old letter, written on a paper towel. It just goes to show that even a deeply flawed parent like me can still be a positive role model.

Dear George,

I'm on the plane to Cancun. I wanted to tell you a few things. First, thank you for everything. Everything is the easiest way to word it because I couldn't begin to count the things you've done for me since I was a nine-year-old little shit with a dirty mouth. Now I'm a twenty-two-year-old little shit, but at least I'm a little more well rounded and a little (very little) more mature. The mouth isn't too bad anymore, either. You've done a good job. I guess military school wasn't necessary after all, huh.

None of us are without fault, but you are a damn good father. I hope one day to be as enthralled with my own children as you are with yours. A lot of people could learn a lot of things from you, and I'm happy to say I have done just that. You've earned more respect with me than anyone else I know.

You may never know how much you've done for me as a person over the years, but I thank you. I hope one day that I can be the father that you are to me and all of us.

I love you.

Your son,
Barry

THE PERFECT DEFAULT

The content of this book literally appears in black and white, but as you know, our day-to-day lives are an amazing mix of those and all the colors in between. But when exploring the challenges—and beauty—of blended families, we cannot do it properly without discussing divorce and its effects on children. With that in mind, as you look ahead at the prospect of starting a new, blended family, make every effort to see it through the eyes of your children. They should be your first—and last—consideration. How will your decisions affect them? What do they have at stake for their future? No matter what, it's all about putting your kids first. When in doubt, put them first. Let it become your perfect default.

ACKNOWLEDGEMENTS

The number of people who were involved in helping to get this finally published is too numerous to list, but I would specifically like to thank my wife, Donna, who made this all possible, and our five children, who preferred to remain nameless, but anyone who knows us knows them as well. I would add, as they do frequently, everything we learned, we learned from them, sometimes painfully all around, and frequently they would need to point things out to us again and again.

In addition I had the support and encouragement of Glen Cambor, MD, Andrea Ferguson White, Roy Aruffo, MD, Joan S. Anderson, PhD, Jean Guez, PhD, Morton Katz, PhD, and Milton Altschuler, MD. A number of different people helped in the reviewing and writing of this including Chris Seger, and Andrew Diamond.

I would add that my wordsmith, and now friend, David Tabatsky, took a jumbled manuscript and turned it into something even my wife would read I would also like to thank our agent, Francine Edelman, and our editors from Skyhorse publishing, Holly Rubino and Amy Li.